E COMMITTED TO OPTIMIZING THE VALUE OF OUR MEMBERS'

D1445014

HE BEST FOOD AND AGRICULTURAL COMPANIES IN THE WORLD.

Celebrating Tradition

BUILDING THE FUTURE

Celebrating Tradition

BUILDING THE FUTURE

SEVENTY-FIVE YEARS OF LAND O'LAKES

Frontispiece

In the late 1920s, an unknown commercial artist created this 3' x 4.5' painting which served as the basis for the redesign of the Land O'Lakes butter carton. The painting's design, as well as that of the subsequent carton, was meant to celebrate the heritage of Minnesota, "the land of 10,000 lakes," from whence Land O'Lakes products came.

©1996
by Land O'Lakes, Inc.
All rights reserved

Printed in Canada

Library of Congress Catalog
Card Number: 95-95304

ISBN 0-9650307-0-9

LAND O LAKES is a registered trademark for products mentioned in this book, including: Sweet Cream Butter, Calf Milk Replacer, Margarine, Country Morning® Blend, 4-Quart® Cheese, No•Fat Sour Cream, Light Sour Cream, Light Butter, Lean Cream, Sour Creme Supreme, and Spread with Sweet Cream.

CONTENTS

Celebrating Tradition ◆ Building The Future

As a grass-roots, democratic organization, Land O'Lakes was founded on the strength, vitality and outright passion of a dedicated group of farmers in 1921. Over the decades, these individuals were joined by thousands of others as the Land O'Lakes family grew and its vision for the future was molded by major events and new opportunities. This book portrays the remarkable story of the people and the activities that have played a role in shaping the history of Land O'Lakes.

Now, at our 75th anniversary, we are intensely focused on the future and on becoming one of the best food and agricultural companies in the world. In the years to come, we will measure our performance by the degree to which we succeed in building a vibrant family farm and cooperative system, as well as strong rural communities.

At the time this organization was being formed, a predecessor of mine, A.J. McGuire, said: "My position is somewhat like that of the Irishman who said he only carried the brick and mortar—the people on the top did all the work. You are the 'people on top' and the building will stand or fall according to how you lay the brick." That sentiment carries the same clear message today.

In recognition, thanks and gratitude, this book is dedicated to the people of Land O'Lakes—members and employees—who have been, and continue to be, the builders of this organization, and who give meaning to our 75th anniversary theme: Celebrating Tradition—Building the Future.

Sincerely,

John E. Gherty
President and Chief Executive Officer

Land O'Lakes was created for a very simple reason: to serve the needs of its members. Back in 1921, those members consisted of co-op creameries in need of a way to improve the quality of their butter, as well as a way to more effectively market and distribute butter to parts of the country where the population was concentrated. The degree to which Land O'Lakes succeeded in meeting those needs is unsurpassed.

Since those early years, much has changed. Advances in technology have transformed the way dairy products are manufactured and distributed. Many of Land O'Lakes original member creameries have transformed themselves into Ag Service cooperatives that handle feed, seed and agronomy products which are supplied through Land O'Lakes. Today, Land O'Lakes members include not only member associations, but also individual farmers and ranchers, who either sell their milk to Land O'Lakes or purchase their Ag Service products directly from it.

What has not changed in the seventy-five years since its founding, though, is Land O'Lakes commitment to meeting member needs. Jim Daniels, board president of the Farmers Cooperative Society of Garner, Klemme and Meservey, Iowa, says: "Co-ops truly are grass-roots organizations that are run for the benefit of all their members." That's what cooperatives are all about, and that's the philosophy to which Land O'Lakes remains committed.

Jim Daniels (left), board president of the Farmers Cooperative Society of Garner, Klemme and Meservey, Iowa; and Sid Heitmeyer, general manager

The Cokato, Minn., co-op creamery, circa 1930

1891—1924

STARTING FROM SCRATCH

1891

1896

1899

Dairying became firmly established in the Upper Midwest by the 1890s. Most milk was produced on family farms, like this one in the St. Croix River Valley, which also raised crops and a host of other livestock.

Minnesota Governor John S. Pillsbury lures Theophilus Levi Haecker, an expert in the science of buttermaking, to the University of Minnesota. Haecker goes on to tour Minnesota's dairy plants and encourages the formation of co-op creameries.

Although often served from beautiful and delicate cut-glass dishes, the unsanitary methods used to produce butter frequently results in a product that "smells bad, tastes worse and does not keep at all," according to the Minnesota Dairy and Food Department.

Less than a decade after his arrival in the state, T.L. Haecker's promotion efforts pay off. The number of co-op creameries in Minnesota skyrockets from two in 1891 to 438 by the end of the decade.

1901

1920

1921

1924

The invention of the hand-operated cream separator allows dairy farmers to more easily skim their own milk, but also attracts large-scale butter manufacturers (or "centralizers") to the Midwest.

John Brandt, a dairy farmer from Litchfield, Minn., wins election as president of the Meeker County Creamery Association, a federation of co-op creameries interested in reducing shipping costs and improving the quality of their butter.

Representatives from 320 of the state's co-op creameries meet in St. Paul on June 7 to form the Minnesota Cooperative Creameries Association. John Brandt is elected to the board of directors.

The association — in need of a catchy trade name to use in marketing members' butter — holds a contest to name the brand. The judges select "Land O'Lakes" from among nearly 100,000 entries.

Off to East Coast markets

Tubs of butter produced at the Milaca, Minn., co-op creamery head to the railroad depot to be shipped east.

MINNESOTA COOPERATIVE CREAMERIES ASSOCIATION

1891—1924

At the end of the nineteenth century, with the United States more than a century old, the American dairy industry was still in its adolescence. Commercial cheese and butter factories had started to appear a few decades earlier. But even as the new century neared, most of the country's butter was produced in home churns. In the Upper Midwest, dairy farming was just beginning to boom — the number of cows in Minnesota tripled between 1860 and 1870. The ways in which farmers produced, shipped and sold their dairy produce, however, had changed little over time. Farmers sold their surplus milk to scattered dairy factories, and the quality and freshness of their milk varied considerably. It was the same story on the farm as well as in the city: Most people who ate butter and cheese were forced to put up with dairy products that "smelt bad, tasted worse and did not keep at all," reported the Minnesota Dairy and Food Department.

Only cooperation among dairy farmers could improve the quality of their product enough to fetch decent prices and attract more customers. So, beginning in the 1890s, farmers started to band together to form jointly operated co-op creameries that produced butter and cheese from the output of the local area's dairy farms. One of the first such cooperative undertakings in Minnesota was in the Danish community of Clark's Grove.

A threat to the cooperatives soon materialized, however: commercial butter manufacturers known as "centralizers." Around the turn of the century, the hand cream separator became common on dairy farms, allowing farmers to skim their own milk. Unlike most co-op creameries, which collected whole milk from farmers and

Turn-of-the-century creameries

Creameries around the turn
of the century accepted deliveries
of milk directly from farmers
(above) and often employed only
two or three people to make
butter or cheese (right).

processed it using centrifugal cream separators, the centralizers accepted hand-skimmed cream. Many cooperative creameries also had to contend with serious financial challenges. Most sold their butter to East Coast middlemen whose prices fluctuated daily — and suspiciously, thought some farmers. Creamery operators believed that the middlemen played games with their shipments, untruthfully claiming the butter arrived in Philadelphia or New York on a day when low prices prevailed. Even if a butter shipment netted a fair price in East Coast markets, the creameries had to pay high rail rates on their less-than-full-carload shipments. On top of it all, many co-ops were unable to get the top prices that premium butter commanded because the centralizers were acquiring the best of the cream.

Enter John Brandt, a dairy farmer from Litchfield, Minn., who brought new ideas and a relentless spirit to the cooperative movement. For several years he had been president of Litchfield's cooperative creamery, but in 1920 he was elected to head the Meeker County Creamery Association, a unique consortium of the area's co-op creameries. Its goal was to improve the quality of the county's butter and to combine butter shipments to the East to save substantially with full-carload rates. Brandt was not satisfied with merely organizing his county's cooperative creameries into an effective shipping unit. He wanted all the creameries to churn their butter from sweet, unsoured cream. Scientists at the U.S. Department of Agriculture had determined that sweet cream butter could be stored longer than butter made from sour cream, and the U.S. Navy was buying sweet cream butter as a provision for long sea voyages. Brandt launched a campaign in Meeker County to teach dairy farmers how to keep their cream from souring, and he encouraged member creameries to pay a 5 percent premium for sweet cream.

But Brandt had an even more ambitious aim. "What dairymen need," he said, "is to get together on a still wider basis, so we can handle the selling of our own products and control their distribution to any market that wants them." If a county-wide cooperative worked in Meeker County, he believed, it would work in all 87 counties of Minnesota. "And then we can do a real job of standardizing, improving, and *selling*," Brandt concluded. That was the spark behind the formation of a true state-wide dairy cooperative organization, the Minnesota Cooperative Creameries Association, which eventually became Land O'Lakes, Inc. Dairy farmers built it from scratch, just as they had their own farms.

The helping hand of science

In 1890 University of Wisconsin professor Stephen M. Babcock invented a process of adding sulphuric acid to milk to more easily measure butterfat content. The process immediately elevated butterfat testing to an exact science.

A wooden creamery churn from before the turn of the century

THEOPHILUS LEVI HAECKER:
A PASSION FOR COOPERATIVES

With his persuasive oratory and striking looks — he had wild black hair and a thick handlebar moustache — Theophilus Levi Haecker probably could have won success as a trial attorney or as a politician. Instead, and to the benefit of dairy farmers everywhere, he devoted his life to the cooperative movement. Born in Ohio and reared on a dairy farm near Cottage Grove, Wis., Haecker actually did begin his career in politics, serving as the private secretary to several Wisconsin governors between 1874 and 1887. His dairy upbringing, however, pulled him to the University of Wisconsin, which, in Madison, operated the world's first school of dairying. His expertise in buttermaking attracted immediate attention, and the University of Minnesota lured him to its agriculture school in 1891.

Once in Minnesota, Haecker learned of an impressive co-op creamery operation in the Danish community of Clark's Grove. He examined it, and the die was cast: For the remainder of his life he preached on behalf of cooperatives throughout the state, eventually becoming known as "the father of co-op creameries." Haecker's evangelism worked — by 1899 there were 438 cooperative creameries in Minnesota. But even after co-op creameries became widespread, Haecker kept working to improve dairying. In the early 1900s, he began a scientific study to determine the effect of different types of feed on butterfat and milk production. Haecker remained vigorous late into life and died at the age of 92 in 1938.

Testing cream at the
Stockholm Cooperative Creamery
in Minnesota

Better feed for better milk

Theophilus L. Haecker spent years devising feeding plans for cows that promised higher outputs of milk.

Train Passes — mementos of Haecker's early Midwest travels

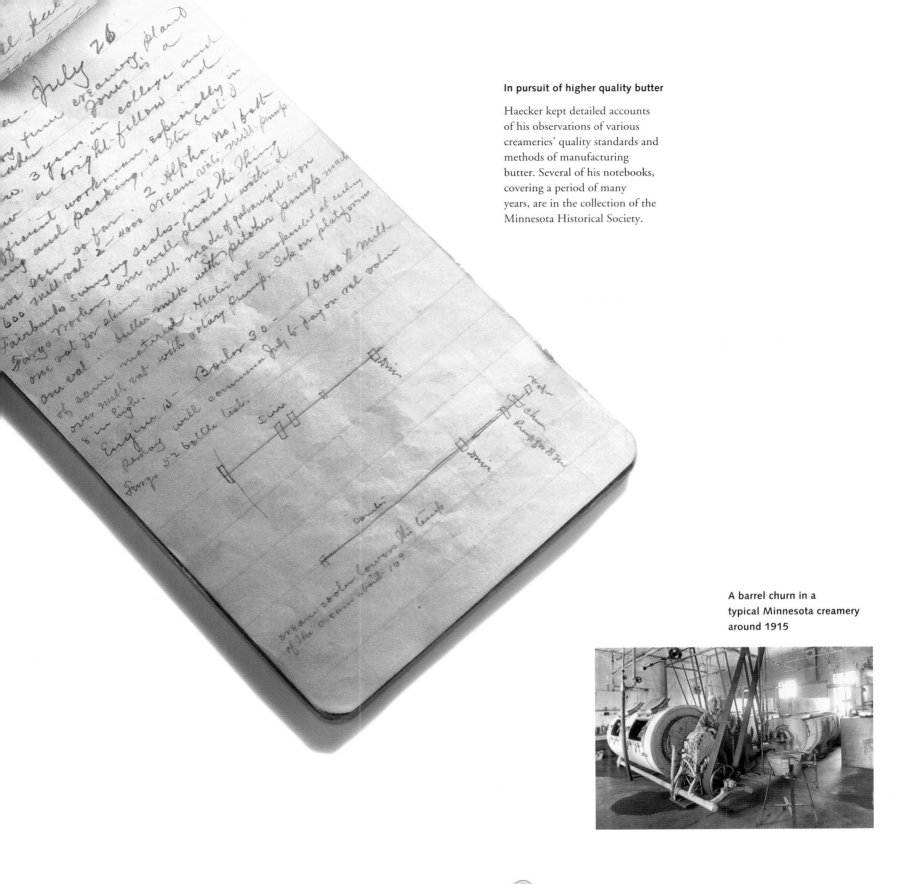

In pursuit of higher quality butter

Haecker kept detailed accounts of his observations of various creameries' quality standards and methods of manufacturing butter. Several of his notebooks, covering a period of many years, are in the collection of the Minnesota Historical Society.

A barrel churn in a typical Minnesota creamery around 1915

The Litchfield Cooperative
Creamery

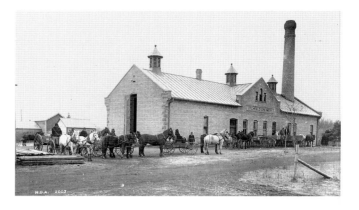

CREAMERIES BAND TOGETHER

By the end of World War I, local dairy cooperatives were well-established in the Upper Midwest. The competition from the privately owned centralizers, however, meant that the co-ops had to run their operations as efficiently as possible. The shipment of butter to the East was one area in which co-ops could trim their costs, and John Brandt of Litchfield became an early exponent of county-wide associations of cooperatives that could fill entire rail cars with tubs of butter at a cost much lower than was required to send many partial-car shipments. In 1920 Brandt was elected president of the Meeker County Creamery Association. It wasn't long before its members were able to save 75 cents per hundred pounds of butter by combining their shipments to the East.

Brandt, Theophilus Haecker, and others believed that a state-wide association of cooperatives could accomplish even more. Marketing Minnesota's butter, improving the quality of dairy products, and boosting the price farmers could receive for their product all became goals of these visionaries. In 1921 representatives from many Minnesota cooperative creameries held meetings to hammer out a plan to form a state-wide organization. On June 7 of that year, after the Minnesota legislature made it legal for individual and county cooperatives to join a larger agency, representatives of 320 of Minnesota's 622 co-op creameries gathered together and voted to form the Minnesota Cooperative Creameries Association. Brandt won election to the board of directors. A new era had begun.

Butter being loaded on train cars
for shipment east

Off to market

A shipment of butter travels from the Milaca Cooperative Creamery to the train station for shipment to Eastern markets. Before the advent of the Minnesota Cooperative Creameries Association and some county-wide associations, individual cooperatives had to pay high rates for the shipment of partial-car lots of butter.

Portrait of a new association

Creamery workers, board members and employees of the Minnesota Cooperative Creameries Association gather for the organization's first group picture in 1922. Arthur McGuire, one of the primary organizers of the association, stands fourth from the right in the front row. He was the association's first general manager.

Early correspondence

During the summer and fall of 1921, the association began a drive to increase its membership, sending letters describing its plans to virtually every cooperative creamery in Minnesota.

AND THE WINNER IS...

At first, the butter supplied by the member creameries and marketed by the association was known as "Minnesota Cooperative Creameries Association Butter." Obviously, there needed to be a catchier brand name. So in 1923 the association launched a highly publicized contest to find a new name for its sweet cream butter. The originators of the top 33 entries would earn a total of $500 in gold — a form of payment suggested by butter's golden color. In addition to running ads throughout Minneapolis and St. Paul promoting the contest, the association assembled every one of its ten trucks in the Twin Cities for a grand parade of vehicles emblazoned with banners crying, "$500 in Gold!"

At the peak of the contest, entries came in from around the country at a rate of 7,000 per day. A panel of judges — they included Minnesota Governor J.A.O. Preus, Minneapolis Mayor George Leach, St. Paul Mayor Arthur Nelson and W.C. Coffey, dean of the University of Minnesota's College of Agriculture — duly assembled to select the winner. Their task was not easy: Nearly 100,000 entries had flooded the association's offices. Many entries were quickly disqualified because other firms owned the trademark or because the names were too similar to others already in use.

On March 25, 1924, the judges reached their final decisions. The runner-up entries were declared to be "Maid O' the West" and "Tommy Tucker." And the winner was... "Land O'Lakes," which suggested the purity and natural beauty of the region in which the association's butter was produced.

Tubs of butter ready for shipment from the Madison, Minn., cooperative creamery in 1923

What's in a name?

An energetic promotional campaign for the contest to name the association's butter drew almost 100,000 entries. Ida Foss of Hopkins, Minn., and George Swift of Minneapolis each received $200. They had submitted the identical name: "Land O'Lakes."

IDA FOSS:
THE WOMAN BEHIND THE NAME "LAND O'LAKES"

In March 1924, a boy drove through deep snowdrifts to get to the home of Ida Foss in Hopkins, Minn. He was bringing big news: The Minnesota Cooperative Creameries Association had just announced the winner of its contest to name its sweet cream butter, and Ida's entry, "Land O'Lakes," had won. Ida and her husband, Edward, were astounded to hear the news. Nearly 100,000 entries had poured into the association's mailbox. The mother of the boy who brought the news had submitted 40 entries, and another contestant had submitted 70 names, but "Land O'Lakes" was Ida's sole contribution. The winning prize was $200 in gold, which both Ida and George Swift of Minneapolis, who had suggested the identical name, received.

Thirty-four years later, after Land O'Lakes had become one of the nation's best-known trade names, Ida told a reporter for *Land O'Lakes News* that her share of the winnings had arrived just in time to pay her taxes. She confessed that Land O'Lakes Sweet Cream Butter was still her favorite, and she believed the name an excellent one. "I have nice memories every time I see or hear the name Land O'Lakes," she said, "and I'm pleased to see the company do so well over the years. I like to think that my name idea had something to do with it."

Pure, fresh and sweet

This brochure, one of the very first to extol the virtues of Land O'Lakes Sweet Cream Butter, focused on the uniqueness of the new butter marketed by the Minnesota Cooperative Creameries Association.

The association wasn't above making lofty claims

Getting the name out

As soon as Land O'Lakes emerged as the new name for the association's sweet cream butter, the association wasted little time using it in ads and promotional materials. Grocery trucks bore banners of the new trademark, and the association's own trucks soon displayed the name along with its new Indian Maiden logo.

It all began with a group of talented and dedicated individuals who recognized the opportunity that marketing sweet cream butter could represent to thousands of dairy farmers who were patrons of Minnesota's co-op creameries. From those early years, when the founders of Land O'Lakes literally changed America's eating habits with the introduction of sweet cream butter, Land O'Lakes has grown into one of the best known, most respected and most successful cooperatives in the nation.

It wasn't long after Land O'Lakes achieved success marketing butter that the organization realized it might be able to do the same with other food products derived from Upper Midwest farms. While Land O'Lakes experienced its share of ups and downs in its subsequent food marketing ventures, it has become firmly established as the premier dairy foods marketing cooperative in the United States. Today it supplies a full line of dairy products — including butter, spreads, cheese and sour creams — to consumer, foodservice and specialty markets across the country.

Tom Martin is the dairy manager for Byerly's grocery store in Chanhassen, Minn. He says that although he determines what products go on Byerly's dairy case shelves, he's merely reflecting the wishes of his customers. "Land O'Lakes has the reputation for quality that our customers look for," he says.

Tom Martin (left), Byerly's dairy manager; and Liz Wilson, Land O'Lakes retail sales representative

A Land O'Lakes butter carton from the early 1930s

1925—1932

EXPANDING HORIZONS

LAND O' LAKES
SWEET CREAM BUTTER
新到美國
蘭來克牛油

●請问後列各大商店購賞
（地　址）

1925   1926   1927

Land O'Lakes Sweet Cream Butter traveled to East Coast markets in a fleet of specially built railroad cars. Unlike most other train cars used for butter transport, these were never used for shipping any other products.

Land O'Lakes signs one of its first contracts for the foreign export of butter. A customer in Africa writes that his shipments of butter survived temperatures of 113° to 122°F: "The taste of the butter in both cases was excellent," he reports.

Positive response to the Land O'Lakes butter name prompts the membership to change the name of the Minnesota Cooperative Creameries Association to Land O'Lakes Creameries, Inc.

Land O'Lakes begins airing its first radio program. Broadcast in the Twin Cities on WCCO, the program features the University of Minnesota School of Agriculture Octette and company President John Brandt, who discusses improvements in butter quality. After the initial broadcast, 1,500 listeners respond with letters.

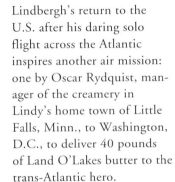

19 27

19 28

19 29

19 30

Lindbergh's return to the U.S. after his daring solo flight across the Atlantic inspires another air mission: one by Oscar Rydquist, manager of the creamery in Lindy's home town of Little Falls, Minn., to Washington, D.C., to deliver 40 pounds of Land O'Lakes butter to the trans-Atlantic hero.

With the dissolution of the Minnesota Cooperative Egg and Poultry Association, Land O'Lakes adds eggs and poultry to its product line. The company at this time is also marketing dressed turkeys and milk powder.

Land O'Lakes opens a Feed department to sell feeds for cattle, hogs, and poultry. Using higher-grade feeds, farmers are able to produce higher quality milk, eggs and poultry that bear the Land O'Lakes label.

As the Great Depression deepens, wholesale butter prices sink to an all-time low. Land O'Lakes steps in to shore up the weakening market by buying 7 million pounds, and within four months, butter prices have edged back up to more than 36 cents per pound.

Champs of the churn

Beginning in 1926, a highlight of Land O'Lakes annual meeting was the bestowal of coveted trophies to the year's best buttermakers.

1925—1932

Soon after the Land O'Lakes name gained acceptance, the butter started winning converts — among them President Calvin Coolidge. The *St. Paul Dispatch* reported that Land O'Lakes butter "has found a permanent place on the President's yacht, the Mayflower, in its cuisine department. A contract was signed last week calling for the delivery of Land O'Lakes Sweet Cream Butter to the steward of the ship, for the use of the Presidential entourage." And not only was the butter of Presidential quality, but it had a distinctive identity. "If thirty-five years ago Minnesota butter was used on the President's table — no one knew of it," the paper continued. "It was just 'butter,' its quality uncertain and its supply equally so."

More and more people were coming to know — and like — Land O'Lakes butter. Production soared 139 percent from 1924 to 1925, and workers in the butter print room were working two shifts, packaging 40,000 lbs. of cartoned butter each day. Five years later, while other dairy producers suffered through the lowest demand in two decades, annual sales of Land O'Lakes butter hit 100 million pounds for the first time. Ironically, the name of the butter had become better known than the name of the organization that produced and marketed it. So another name change seemed in order. At the organization's 1926 annual meeting, Minnesota Cooperative Creameries Association officially became Land O'Lakes Creameries, Inc. The 3,000 members in attendance unanimously approved the change.

Making the most of the growing recognition of its brand name, Land O'Lakes aggressively sought out new markets for its products. For starters, it successfully courted large grocery store chains — particularly in the eastern United States. The 1926 introduction of Land O'Lakes butter to Fisher Brothers stores in Cleveland produced an increase in the grocery firm's sales of one-pound packages from 1 percent of total butter sales to 35 percent.

Bringing news to members

From its first issue in January 1925, *Land O'Lakes News* communicated important information to members, including product prices and the sales advances made by the company's representatives out East.

"With your co-operation," the Fisher Brothers owners wrote to Land O'Lakes, "we feel sure we can make this 90 percent within four months." At another grocery chain, H.T. Brockelman in Massachusetts, the high quality of Land O'Lakes butter caused butter sales to rise 50 percent. And after two years of effort, the company in 1930 signed on New York's largest food chain, the James Butler Co., to carry Land O'Lakes butter. One-pound packages of butter were responsible for most of these sales coups, and the old 50-pound butter tub — a fixture in America's grocery stores for decades — was rapidly becoming a rarity. By 1929, single-pound cartons accounted for 30 percent of Land O'Lakes butter sales, and a new one-pound parchment-wrapped butter roll, introduced the previous year, contributed its share.

The company's foreign sales were growing, as well. In 1925, Land O'Lakes teamed with an importer in Lima, Peru, to distribute 500,000 pounds of butter in the Spanish-speaking countries of Latin America. Soon sweet cream butter, complete with Spanish text on the packaging, appeared on store shelves in Mexico, Panama, Venezuela, Colombia, and Peru. And arrangements with other importers brought Land O'Lakes butter to Haiti, the British West Indies, and the Philippines. In 1927, a Boston man notified the company that he had found Land O'Lakes butter for sale in a small town in Japan, and an American minister in China reported seeing a package in a shop in the city of Suifu, 1,800 miles up the Yangtze River from the port of Shanghai.

By this time, some people would go to any lengths to get their hands on Land O'Lakes butter, and member creameries began finding themselves the victims of butterfat thieves. In 1926, the company placed this notice in several Minneapolis-St. Paul newspapers: "$200 reward will be paid by Land O'Lakes Creameries, Inc., to the person or persons furnishing information leading to the arrest and conviction of the persons who robbed the Randall Co-operative Creamery on the night of April 27, 1926." Eventually four thieves and fences were arrested. In 1932, a Chicago man was sentenced to five years in prison for stealing 500 pounds of butter, five cases of eggs, and 199 pounds of cheese from the creamery in Monticello, Minn. One can only assume he thought it was worth the risk.

Courting the chains

During the late 1920s, Land O'Lakes built solid relationships with several grocery chains.

A line-up of trucks outside of Land O'Lakes Detroit, Mich., office

First one out of the chute

Very few examples remain today of this packaging milestone from the mid 1920s — the first butter box to bear the Land O'Lakes name. Within four years, the box was redesigned to show more of the Indian Maiden (facing the viewer) and less of the Minnesota-inspired scenery.

Reaching a mass audience

In 1930, Land O'Lakes began an ambitious ad campaign in *Good Housekeeping* magazine, the first national advertising program that an American butter marketer had ever launched. The ads repeatedly pointed to 100 percent sweet cream as the main ingredient in Land O'Lakes butter.

**Don't forget it's SWEET
(not sour) cream**

The debut ad in Land O'Lakes *Good Housekeeping* campaign of the early '30s (lower left) featured a butter roll, while a later one (lower right) highlighted the butter's inspection and seal of approval from the U.S. Department of Agriculture. These ads and other marketing efforts spelled the end of the big 50-pound butter tub that long occupied a spot near the main counter of America's grocery stores. Consumers as well as grocers came to prefer the one-pound packages and quarter-pound sticks.

JOHN BRANDT:
FROM DAIRY FARMER TO NATIONAL LEADER

At age 34, John Brandt was one of the youngest men involved in organizing what was to eventually become Land O'Lakes. He already had a reputation around his hometown of Litchfield, Minn., for being a go-getter, and had been made president of his local co-op creamery because his fellow dairymen wanted to harness at least some of his boundless energy to their collective advantage.

In the Spring of 1924, Brandt traveled to New York City to try and drum up butter business for the fledgling Minnesota Cooperative Creameries Association. After being rebuffed by a number of the butter wholesalers who had traditionally handled Midwestern dairy products, Brandt decided to switch tactics and call directly on retailers themselves. He met with dozens of chain store representatives and food manufacturers, not only in New York City, but also in Boston, Buffalo, Cleveland, Pittsburgh, Philadelphia and Chicago. Brandt ended up

selling 40 million pounds of co-op-churned butter as a result of his trip, and ushered in a new system of selling and shipping butter directly to retailers, thus bypassing middlemen and increasing profits for Midwest dairy producers. Brandt went on to become both board president and general manger of Land O'Lakes. He was an articulate spokesman for dairy farmers and the dairy industry, and a tireless promoter of agricultural self-help.

Brandt collapsed and died on March 4, 1953, just after completing a fiery speech to members of the co-op creamery in Middle River, Minn. He was eulogized as "a giant among men." But to most, he was simply "Mr. Land O'Lakes."

A Winter delivery

Unloading butter from boat-- New York City

Prof. Haecker --father of co-operative creameries in Minnesota

Land O'Lakes everywhere

During the '20s and '30s, Land O'Lakes promoted itself in many ways other than through traditional advertising. It produced a film strip detailing its history (top), produced promotional photos of children at play with Land O'Lakes-derived toys, and splashed its name across the sides of trucks.

LAND O'LAKES
Sweet Cream
BUTTER
Churned from SWEET instead of sour CREAM

BUTTER-EGGS-POULTRY-CHEESE-DRIED MILK.

Loaf of bread containing
sweet buttermilk powder.

Face forward

The first redesign of the Land O'Lakes butter carton in 1928 oriented the Maiden to face the viewer, with the fertile valleys and pure waters of the Upper Midwest in the background.

A new home

Members at Land O'Lakes 1925 annual meeting voted to build a new organizational headquarters. Construction began on September 1, 1925, and six months later Land O'Lakes had a new home in Northeast Minneapolis.

THE GROWING ENTERPRISE MOVES

"Cooperative marketing," declared Minnesota Governor Theodore Christianson at the dedication of Land O'Lakes new headquarters in Northeast Minneapolis in 1926, "has passed its infancy and is now in the stage of fighting maturity." Just as Land O'Lakes acquired a new corporate name and was meeting success in marketing its growing line of butter, poultry and eggs, it built for itself a home that provided breathing room, up-to-date equipment and laboratory facilities, and ample warehouse capacity. This building was to play host to the company's expansion and remain a community landmark for more than 45 years.

The organization's first two headquarters, modest offices and warehouses rented in St. Paul, had been quickly outgrown. Even by 1925, when the old butter print room was working two shifts and pushing through 40,000 pounds of butter a day, all of the packing work was done by hand. John Brandt and other Land O'Lakes officers occasionally had to pitch in to help with rush orders. The new facility, with its automated packaging equipment, ended all of that and greatly increased the volume of butter that could be processed in the print room. Every year the building housed Land O'Lakes large annual meetings, and it became a must stop for agriculturally-minded visitors in the Twin Cities — whether they were from Duluth or Scandinavia.

Inside the office portion of Land O'Lakes new headquarters

State of the art

Employees in the new building's butter print room worked with packaging equipment that was then the height of automation.

BEN ZAKARIASEN:
A RESEARCHER AND A GENTLEMAN

Mold may not be of interest to everyone, but to Ben Zakariasen it was both fascinating and troublesome. Zakariasen first began working at Land O'Lakes in the 1920s, while a student at the University of Minnesota. A brilliant agricultural researcher, he was hired to set up the company's first laboratory. His assignment was to study methods of improving dairy products.

At that time, mold and yeast infestations were a problem for many creameries. Tubs of butter would sprout unsightly growths long before they should have spoiled, and even invisible spores could affect the taste. Zakariasen devoted a great deal of time studying the problem, and he determined that contaminated piping was the source of the mold and yeast.

In a series of articles in *Land O'Lakes News*, Zakariasen detailed how creamery operators could protect their butter from contamination. Land O'Lakes found and began to sell piping that creameries could take apart and more easily sterilize. For the next 40 years, Zakariasen led the company's efforts to improve its products. Research eventually became the domain of a large department that focused on animal feeds and other agricultural products, as well as dairy foods.

Land O'Lakes butter makes the grade

Land O'Lakes took the unprecedented step of asking the U.S. Department of Agriculture for assistance in determining the best way to grade butter. As a result, the company launched a grading program in cooperation with federal and state inspectors and became the first butter manufacturer to earn a seal of quality from the government agency.

CERTIFIED BUTTER

We certify that this butter is made entirely of fresh, pasteurized sweet cream, produced by herds tested for Tuberculosis. This package of butter contains a "Certificate of Quality" which certifies that it was graded by a Butter Grader of the U. S. Department of Agriculture and Minnesota Department of Agriculture and scored 93 points.

Butter to score 93 points must be FINE, SWEET and CLEAN in flavor and perfect in respect to body, color, salt and package.

LAND O'LAKES CREAMERIES, Inc.
MINNEAPOLIS, MINNESOTA

Creamery labs improve

Member creameries continued to improve the quality of their labs due to the influence of Land O'Lakes. This is the lab at the Watertown, Minn., creamery.

Room for research

Land O'Lakes new Northeast Minneapolis headquarters included the organization's first area dedicated solely to dairy research.

A member's badge from
Land O'Lakes 10th annual
meeting in 1931

A cast of thousands

As Land O'Lakes grew, its
annual meetings of members
swelled into assemblies of 3,000
or more people. The new
headquarters, with its vast
warehouse space, could finally
accommodate that many people.

Butter grading

Grading contests held in conjunction with the annual meeting determined the years' top buttermakers.

Now that's cooperation

A long-standing tradition of the annual meetings was the lunch, prepared for the thousands of attendees by employees and their spouses and family members. "Over 3,000 people were served without a hitch in less than three-quarters of an hour and were all ready to go back to work," wrote one observer of an early annual meeting.

A name that means quality

Member creameries soon learned the value of close identification with the Land O'Lakes name.

Etched in glass

Member creameries began placing the Land O'Lakes logo on their milk bottles in the late 1920s.

This is a Land O'Lakes creamery

By the early 1930s, hundreds of red, white and blue enamel Land O'Lakes creamery signs were proudly displayed on co-op creameries throughout the Upper Midwest.

The name that builds business

The 1920s saw creameries boasting of their Land O'Lakes affiliation in ads and other promotional materials.

YOU
Always Get Best Results
when you bring
your cream
to the
Land O' Lakes Creamery

THE HOME OF SWEET CREAM BUTTER

We wish to thank our patrons for the loyal support and co-operation given, that has made possibe our making the famous Land O' Lakes Butter. Join hands with your neighbor in this great marketing program.

Stockholm
Co-Operative Creamery Association

Elmer Morris, pres.   O. T. Munson, secty.
J. A. Ekstrand, vice pres. J. O. Grundahl, treas.
A. L. Johnson   Gust Peterson
          J. Arthur Anderson

Colorful bottlecaps

Creameries discovered the popularity of chocolate milk in the 1920s and '30s, creating a variety of colorful "pogs" for the tops of their bottles.

Diversification increases opportunity

Land O'Lakes entry into egg marketing and other poultry-related businesses in the late '20s opened up opportunities for feed sales.

ENTRY INTO AG SERVICES

Land O'Lakes entered the dairy equipment business in 1925, offering cooling tanks, butter weighing stands, pumps, motors and cream cans to members. It did not take much time for additional agricultural product sales to expand, however. Soon, with the realization that better feed would improve farmers' milk and cream yields, the organization began producing and selling cattle feed. Land O'Lakes increasing involvement in turkey and egg production in the late 1920s made poultry feed a natural extension of the line, as well. And soon hog feed was also featured in the Land O'Lakes catalogue. To supplement the feed, seed and equipment now for sale, the company offered members advice on how to effectively raise livestock and establish proper feeding programs.

A familiar face on a new package

The Land O'Lakes trademark appeared on sacks of animal feed beginning in 1929. Company brochures relayed the latest "scientific" feeding and management practices.

It was only logical that some eight years after it was established as a butter marketing organization, Land O'Lakes expanded its vision and became involved in the manufacture and distribution of feed. After all, proper feed and feeding methods are essential for quality milk and butter production.

Although Land O'Lakes today is one of the foremost feed companies in the nation, involved in everything from cattle, hog, poultry and specialty feeds to milk replacers, it's undergoing a transformation in its approach to the feed business. Land O'Lakes is moving from being just a feed company into becoming an animal production system — intent on helping livestock producers raise exactly the types of animals customers want. This transformation involves the channeling of research dollars into proprietary and branded products, with the focus on lean market animals in swine, and on high-producing cows in dairy.

Andy Dejno is a third-generation dairyman who milks cows and raises dairy steers on his farm near Mondovi, Wis. Dejno says there's lots of competition for his feed business in the area, but he chooses to do business with a Land O'Lakes-affiliated co-op — Co-op Equity in Mondovi — because of the quality of their products, the quality of their service and because they are a cooperative. "Farmers were wise to have built a co-op system like this," Dejno says. "Farmers are stronger standing together than if we had to stand alone."

Jim Connolly (left), Livestock Production Specialist; and Andy Dejno, a dairy farmer from Mondovi, Wis.

A percale Land O'Lakes feed bag from the 1940s

1933—1946

YEARS OF DANGER

| 1933 | 1934 | 1937 |

By 1934, 30,000 retailers across the country carried Land O'Lakes products. Many placed the Land O'Lakes logo on their delivery trucks. These trucks and drivers are lined up outside of Land O'Lakes Detroit sales office.

In a year of severe financial depression and federally ordered bank holidays, Land O'Lakes issues scrip money — fully backed by the organization's own financial resources — to help member co-ops pay their dairy producers.

Members of Wisconsin's National Cheese Producers Federation join Land O'Lakes, bringing the organization its first significant work in grading and marketing cheese.

Land O'Lakes opens its first milk-drying plant in Luck, Wis. The facility manufactures skim milk powder, casein and buttermilk powder — all products that would figure prominently in the war that looms ahead.

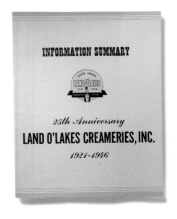

1940	**19**42	**19**44	**19**46
Using Mississippi River bluff limestone caves, Land O'Lakes begins production of aged blue cheese and a new Roquefort-style cheese that it will eventually market under the name "Cavqurd" — pronounced "cave-cured."	Land O'Lakes converts many of its plants to produce such essential war goods as dried eggs and milk, poultry, and butter for overseas military use.	By this time, Land O'Lakes ranks as the nation's largest producer of dry milk powder. Production soars from 22 million pounds to 119 million pounds in four years.	Land O'Lakes celebrates its Silver Anniversary. At the 25th Annual Meeting, Dr. J.O. Christianson, head of the University of Minnesota ag school, praises the founders of Land O'Lakes as "translators of dreams into reality."

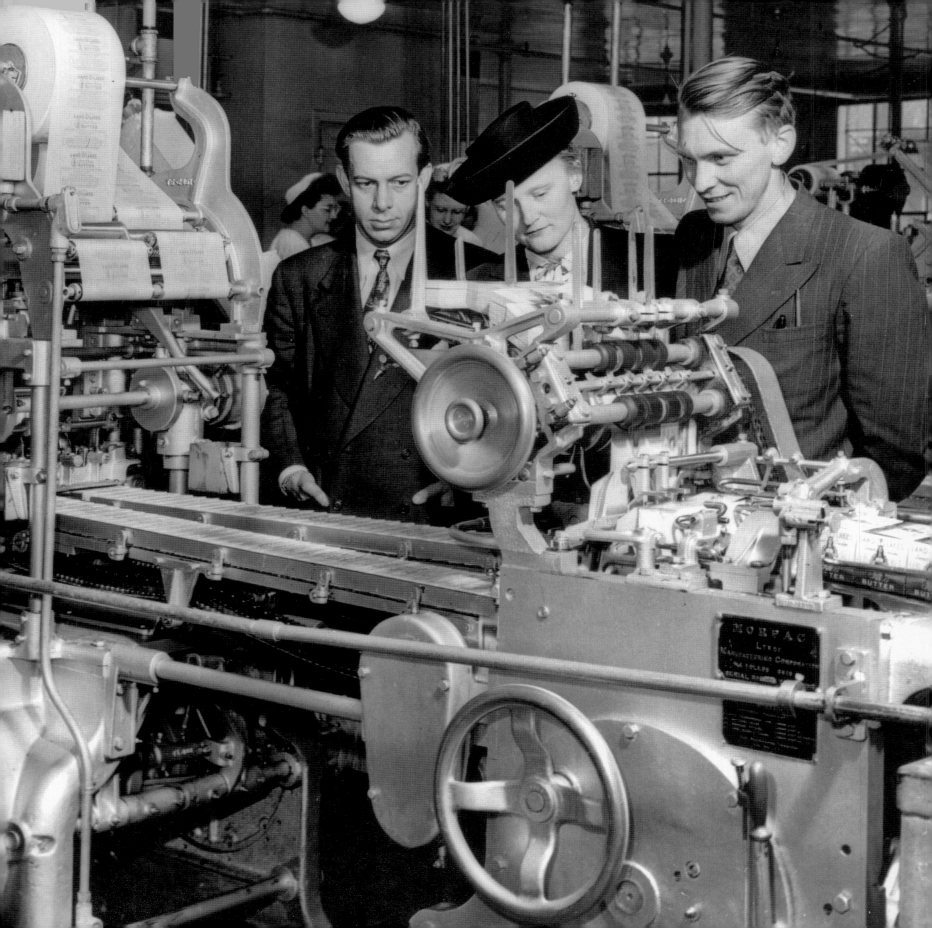

Admirers from afar

Norwegian visitors, along with
an official from the Office of War
Information (left), inspect
Land O'Lakes automated butter
packaging equipment during
the height of World War II.

1933—1946

Viewed from afar, the years of the Great
Depression and World War II might appear to have been spirited times for Land
O'Lakes — just a continuation of the years of exciting growth that the organization experienced in the late 1920s. Many things did press forward normally: Customers sent in butter wrappers to receive such premiums as Hiawatha pattern
silverware; the poet Edgar A. Guest and singer Eddy Howard teamed up to promote Land
O'Lakes in a radio show that was broadcast around the country; and the Land O'Lakes
kitchens merrily turned out such recipes as the one for "cottage cheese temptation," a combination of bread, cottage cheese, butter, green peppers, and tomato soup.

Even after the war broke out, some GIs sent back letters mentioning little of fear and bat-
tle — but professing a longing for . . . dairy products. "I like it here fine. It is a great country, but I want to show the
folks here what really good cheese tastes like," wrote army private Lawrence E. Bisbee in 1942 from Anchorage, Alaska,
to his aunt in St. Paul. "Will you please send me a pound of Land O'Lakes cheese?" When the cheese arrived six weeks
later, Bisbee appreciatively wrote back that "I got all the Minnesota fellows in my barracks together and we cut up the
pound of cheese so that each one of us had a bite. And did it taste good! Like home!"

Despite this outward cheerfulness and optimism, however, these were dangerous years for
Land O'Lakes and for the country. Land O'Lakes managed to weather the Depression quite well, strengthened by an ad
campaign that emphasized the nutritional value of dairy products and a diversification plan that made the company a
producer and marketer of eggs, turkeys, dry milk and casein — as well as its mainstay, butter. But the outbreak of war
altered Land O'Lakes long-range plans virtually overnight. Food shortages wreaked havoc upon America's eating habits,
and the government laid claim to huge amounts of domestically produced foodstuffs for military consumption. The

price of butter shot up to $1 a pound, giving oleo margarine and other forms of "artificial butter" a tremendous boost.

Between 1941 and 1946, the nation's per-capita consumption of butter fell by 57 percent. While in 1939 the University of Minnesota football team could proudly report its annual gobbling up of 600 pounds of Land O'Lakes butter — 10 pounds a day during early practice sessions — the passage of just four years transformed butter into a rationed item that visitors to the Minnesota State Fair hungrily viewed through glass cases in front of the Land O'Lakes display. Temporarily replacing butter as Land O'Lakes growth product was powdered milk, which the military sought in almost limitless quantities. The company produced 940 million pounds of dairy foods, eggs, turkey, and chicken during the war years, much of it for the armed forces. One Land O'Lakes producer, Harold Zupp of Albert Lea, Minn., raised a single turkey flock in 1944 that provided Thanksgiving dinners for 100,000 GIs.

While helping the armed forces wage war in Europe and the Pacific, Land O'Lakes was fighting its own battle at home. Price controls and rationed supplies brought troubles to many American farmers, and some spoke out in favor of adjustments to the government controls. In response, opponents (including some members of Congress) called the farmers traitors. Land O'Lakes created a series of ads promoting farmers as hard workers for the war effort. One ad titled "The Greatest Mass Production Job in History" drew national praise. "I have heard more favorable comment from members of the House Committee on Agriculture in connection with your ad...than of any other recent article," wrote U.S. Representative Victor Wickersham of Oklahoma. "I wish that more of the people understood their subject as well as you do."

Nobody laughed at this funny money

When President Franklin Roosevelt declared a "bank holi-day," Land O'Lakes issued thousands of dollars of temporary scrip currency that it replaced with real cash once the banks reopened.

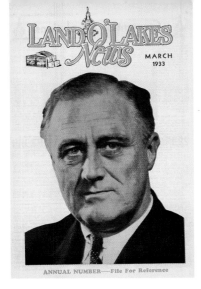

The New Deal in Land O'Lakes News

Franklin Roosevelt's inauguration as President drew recognition on the cover of *Land O'Lakes News*.

Cool heads in hard times

Land O'Lakes President John Brandt, seated sixth from the right, together with his fellow board members in 1934: Archie Brovold, Stuart McLeod, Frank White, Herman Berg, J.H. Reil, Frank Farley, Chris Skaar, H.A. Illsley, E.M. Rosenberg, A.L. Veigel, Oscar A. Berning, C.A. Torkelson, J.O. Bjorklund, C.J. Le Count, E.O. Melsness, Vern Lockwood, John B. Irwin, Jens Jensen, Fred W. Huntzicker, A.L. Berg, Elmer W. Wicks, and C.J. Thomson.

EDNA McKENNA:
AT WORK IN THE BUTTER PRINT ROOM

Edna McKenna was a recent high school graduate with part-time experience as a department store sales clerk when she began a 30-year-long career at Land O'Lakes Northeast Minneapolis headquarters in 1940. "My cousin worked there, and she told me they were hiring," McKenna remembers. "First I started wrapping butter by hand. Then they put me on the chiplet machine, which made the little pats of butter for restaurants. Later I operated the machine that wrapped pounds of butter, then the one that wrapped quarters. I enjoyed it. I got to work just about every machine in the print room, and we all had a lot of friends."

At first, McKenna lived on 24th Avenue N.E. in Minneapolis, a couple of miles from the plant. She walked to work, usually making her return trip faster when she received her weekly paycheck and was eager to spend her earnings, she recalls. That first year, her take home pay for 40 hours of work was $17.49. "That was good money at the time — I felt rich," she says. "I took the check and was able to go downtown to buy dresses, shoes and a hat for under $10. I had to pay room and board at home, but I still had $5 left over."

McKenna has good memories of her life at Land O'Lakes. "It was a good job. Even now I always buy Land O'Lakes butter, because all the years I worked with it, I knew it was good."

New packaging equipment impresses visitors to Land O'Lakes

Technology wins out

Despite the financial challenges of the Depression, Land O' Lakes continued adding to the technological sophistication of its facilities. New equipment in the butter print room, introduced in 1935, further automated the process of packing, labeling and boxing cartons of butter.

4000 years in the making

Land O'Lakes magazine advertising in the mid 1930s continued to emphasize the distinctive taste of sweet cream butter, but also highlighted the nutritional benefits of dairy foods.

4000 YEARS

...the World waited for this new and different kind of *Butter*

DISCOVERY OF BUTTER, according to Hindu tradition, was made by an Aryan warrior more than forty centuries ago. Riding with a goatskin of milk before him, the milk soured and the horse's gallop churned it to butter.

THE PRIMITIVE CHURN was a skin filled with sour whole milk, hung up and shaken until the butter separated. Arab women still use this method.

BUTTER is one of the earliest foods named in the Bible. Abraham served it to heavenly guests. (Genesis 18:8)

Butter, churned from fresh
SWEET (INSTEAD OF SOUR) CREAM

EACH CHURNING OF LAND O'LAKES sweet-cream butter is tested and graded by a U. S. gov't grader. The *Certificate of Quality* in every package is authorized by the U. S. Dept. of Agriculture.

MOST BUTTER is churned from sour cream because of the difficulty and cost of keeping cream sweet until it can be churned.

YOU'LL never know how good hot biscuits or new garden peas can be . . . until you've enjoyed the treats they become with butter churned from *fresh*, sweet cream. Ask your grocer today for LAND O' LAKES *sweet-cream* butter.

THE FRESH, delicious flavor of LAND O'LAKES *sweet-cream* butter is due to the sweet cream from which it is churned—rushed *fresh* to creameries from 95,000 farms.

NOT ONE DROP of sour cream is ever used in LAND O'LAKES butter. Every gallon must pass rigid tests for freshness, flavor and richness before it is accepted.

A miniature pictorial history of butter, in colors, mailed FREE. Write to Land O'Lakes Creameries, Inc., 1153 N'western Bank Bldg., Minneapolis

LAND O'LAKES
Sweet Cream BUTTER

LAND O'LAKES SWEET CREAM BUTTER

ACCEPTED AMERICAN MEDICAL ASSN. Committee on Foods

The ACCEPTED seal of the Am. Medical Assn. Committee on Foods on every package.

Caves of Cheese

In 1934 two large cheese producers joined Land O'Lakes: the National Cheese Producers Federation and the Minnesota Cheese Producers Association. Instantly, Land O'Lakes cheese marketing efforts expanded, and the organization began placing heavier emphasis on cheese research and development. A 10-million-cubic-foot chain of limestone caves along the Mississippi River bluffs in St. Paul, where the temperature and humidity remained constant year-round, became the site of experiments in cheese aging.

Window Displays

As Land O'Lakes various cheeses gained wider distribution, retailers began displaying them in store windows.

A new type of ad for Land O'Lakes

Land O'Lakes magazine ads began spotlighting cheese in the mid 1930s after two large cheese producers joined the organization in 1934.

A Land O'Lakes cheese box from the 1930s

A slug used in the typesetting of one of Land O'Lakes early cheese advertisements

Expanding on the name

This photograph, taken from a 1935 cookbook, shows a small portion of the growing line of Land O'Lakes food products.

A NAME TO BE RECKONED WITH

Back in the mid 1920s, the Land O'Lakes name first appeared on butter. Then the Minnesota Cooperative Creameries Association renamed itself after its popular brand. During the next decade, the company made the most of its lucrative trademark, introducing an entirely new family of merchandise — both food products and Agricultural Services items — that bore the Land O'Lakes name and carried the image of the Indian Maiden. There was Land O'Lakes Fly Spray, which, according to the company's literature, "will not blister, will not taint the milk and will both kill and repel flies." 1933 saw the introduction of Land O'Lakes salt indicator, acid indicator, casein glue, sterilizer, butter color, and cream neutralizer — products primarily made for use by creameries. Land O'Lakes maple syrup followed in 1934, and eventually such Land O'Lakes products as floor wax, eggs, condensed milk, salad dressings, mayonnaise, ice cream and casein paint, as well as an expanded line of hog, cattle and poultry feeds, hybrid seeds, and other farm supplies.

A label from a barrel of dried skim milk

Some of the many Land O'Lakes products available in the 1930s

Pictured on the following page are a few of the literally dozens of Land O'Lakes-labeled products available during the mid 1930s. Some were produced and packaged by member creameries and sold locally — like ice cream. Others — like flour and paint — were sold by Land O'Lakes to a wide audience, but actually manufactured and packaged in Land O'Lakes-identified containers by other companies. The stoneware butter crock was an early example of reusable packaging. Empty crocks, decorated either with the Land O'Lakes trademark or with the name of a member creamery, could be obtained from a local creamery and refilled any number of times with freshly churned butter simply by returning it to the creamery.

PATRICK McRAITH:
A DEPRESSION-ERA DAIRY FARMER

Pat McRaith remembers the terribly hot summer of 1936, which he spent working his family dairy farm near Hutchinson, Minn. "One day the temperature came in at 105 degrees," he says. "I had to chase a horse around all day, and afterward I just jumped into a tub of cold water. I had a nosebleed, and I was completely all in. I suppose it was a dangerous thing to do."

McRaith started farming in 1930, when he was in his late teens. "Those days we used to pitch hay all summer," he says. "There was no refrigeration, and we had to smoke our meat in a smokehouse. That's all my mother did during the summer — get everything settled in the cellar and fill the basement with canned goods for the winter. We grew all our own food. The only thing we bought in stores was crackers for the soup." McRaith says dairy farming in the 1930s could be scary. "Creditors would come in the middle of the night and rap

on the door. They'd say, 'Get out by tomorrow, we're taking over.' An awful lot of people lost their farms." Poor roads were another challenge McRaith faced. "The roads were not made for trucks," he recalls. "The township roads weren't plowed during the winter, but we still had to get our milk out. State Highway 15 (about a mile east of McRaith's farm) was the only highway that stayed open, and it took four to five guys just to keep the milk cans from tipping over getting there."

McRaith occasionally traveled to the Hutchinson Cooperative Creamery, where he sold his milk, to hear John Brandt speak. "That Brandt, he could talk," McRaith says. "He could talk fast, but he had his feet on the ground, he knew what he was talking about — even when people would get up and argue with him."

A hired hand on the McRaith dairy farm

Meal ticket for Ag Services

Land O'Lakes Calf Meal, a product introduced during the 1930s, was evidence of the gradual expansion of Agricultural Services into an important segment of the organization's business.

Changes on the farm

The Agricultural Services department of Land O'Lakes commanded a relatively small share of the company's total business at the time of America's entry into World War II — between 5 and 10 percent. But its activity was picking up.

Land O'Lakes realized that it could further aid its members by supplying quality ag inputs to farmers, as well as serving as a vehicle for marketing their farm products. So the selection of Land O'Lakes feed products was expanded and hybrid seeds were introduced.

A boy of 11 aids in the war effort on his family's farm near Winona, Minn.

An "E" for excellence

Land O'Lakes took great pride in 1944 when its dry milk plant in Whitehall, Wis., won a prestigious Army-Navy E Award.

In the army now

Walter Cantley was one of hundreds of Land O'Lakes employees who shipped off to war.

"He says he's bored with these small shipments—he used to check Land O'Lakes Sweet Cream Butter sales!"

Ads to keep the name alive

With the rationing of butter during the war, Land O'Lakes sometimes had precious little to offer the civilian public. Its long-time ad agency, Campbell-Mithun, developed a clever series of cartoon advertisements that kept readers interested. A 1943 survey by the American Newspaper Publishers Association pronounced them to be the most widely read ads ever recorded.

VICTORY VIA DRIED MILK

Dried milk, primarily a baking ingredient in the 1930s, grew into a blockbuster military provision during World War II — and Land O'Lakes emerged as the world's biggest manufacturer. Armed forces surveys showed that milk was the favorite beverage of 70 percent of the fighting forces, and yet fluid milk was impossibly bulky and too prone to spoilage for shipment thousands of miles overseas. Powdered milk provided an easy solution to the problem.

Land O'Lakes creameries had first experimented with drying buttermilk in 1926. Soon after, member creameries began using new techniques to dry whole and skim milk — the latter previously used only for animal feed. Land O'Lakes built its first milk-drying plant in 1937 in Luck, Wis., and by the peak war years another 21 plants were in operation in the Upper Midwest. The increase in demand for dried milk was phenomenal — growing from 22 million pounds in 1941 to 119 million pounds in 1945. After the war, Land O'Lakes dried milk became an important ingredient in formulas developed to help malnourished refugees and concentration camp survivors, and the company worked hard to discover new uses and markets for this versatile product.

Honoring the soldiers

Land O'Lakes erected a tribute to its employees who were serving in the armed forces during World War II.

ROLL OF HONOR
EMPLOYEES OF THE LAND O'LAKES CREAMERIES, INC. NOW SERVING IN THE ARMED FORCES OF THE UNITED STATES

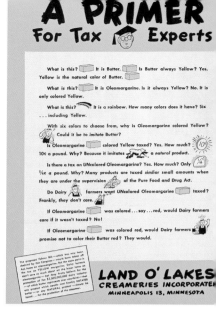

The oleo tax issue

The degree of Land O'Lakes opposition to repeal of the colored oleo tax is reflected in this ad which appeared in *Land O'Lakes News*.

SILVER ANNIVERSARY CELEBRATION

1946 marked not only the first year of the post-war era, but also Land O'Lakes Silver Anniversary. The company had racked up many achievements during its first 25 years: more than $1 billion in sales, the creation of new standards of butter quality, innovative packaging, the breaking of old and inefficient distribution patterns, and pioneering efforts to improve dairy production on farms and in creameries. Along the way, Land O'Lakes had become the world's largest producer of powdered milk and had nurtured the most highly respected brand name in the dairy business.

"The facts remain," President John Brandt said at the organization's 25th annual meeting, "that Land O'Lakes Creameries enjoys a recognition locally, nationally and internationally of leadership...[and] has brought about a decided betterment of financial and other conditions for the dairy farmers of America." Dr. J.O. Christianson, head of the University of Minnesota School of Agriculture and also a speaker at the 25th anniversary celebration, put it more succinctly: "The founders of Land O'Lakes were the translators of dreams into reality."

Land O'Lakes trucks outside the organization's Chicago offices, circa 1946

A book to remember

Kenneth Ruble, a writer with a distinguished and varied career in journalism and business writing, was hired to mark Land O'Lakes 25th anniversary celebration with the publication of his book *Men to Remember*. It chronicled the history of Land O'Lakes, from the dawn of Midwest cooperatives through the start of the post-war era. Ruble went on to work for Campbell-Mithun, the ad agency that handled the Land O'Lakes account, and to write *Farmers Make it Happen*, the history of Land O'Lakes first 50 years.

Men to Remember

by Kenneth D. Ruble

Land O'Lakes involvement in seed goes way back to 1929 with the establishment of a small seed sales operation geared to supplying seed to member creameries that were just then entering the ag supply business. It took until the 1970s, however, and the tremendous expansion of Ag Services, brought about by the merger with Felco, for the Seed division to begin to take on the importance it holds within Land O'Lakes today.

Although smaller, in terms of annual sales, than either the Agronomy Company or the Feed division, the Land O'Lakes Seed division plays an important role in providing Ag Service member accounts a complementary ag product line. Concentrating on alfalfa, soybean and corn varieties, the Seed division is committed to delivering the latest technologies as well as the top performing genetics to its co-op members. Examples of such products include multi-leaf alfalfas, energy-dense corn and new insect-resistant crop varieties.

Gerald Helling, a LaSalle, Minn., farmer, says: "I appreciate how well my cooperative's Seed and Agronomy departments work together to recommend the proper seed varieties for my farm, based on soil variation and fertility." It's that kind of synergy that makes the Seed division such an important part of the total ag supply picture at Land O'Lakes.

Gerald Helling (left), a farmer from LaSalle, Minn.; and Howard Brekke, agronomist, LaSalle Farmers Grain Co.

A 1950s bag of Land O'Lakes alfalfa seed

1947—1962

A MANDATE TO DIVERSIFY

1948

1950

1951

Consumer sales of Land O'Lakes butter plunged 57 percent during the Second World War due to high prices and government rationing. After the war, billboards like this one reminded shoppers of Land O'Lakes "Extra Good Taste," and by 1948, Land O'Lakes butter sales returned to their pre-war levels.

Land O'Lakes opens its first research test farm, in Anoka, Minn. Scientists use the 187-acre experimental farm to test animal feeds, fertilizers, and seeds.

The United States Congress passes the Margarine Act, which repeals federal restrictions on the coloring of margarine. Land O'Lakes butter sales fall 17 percent in the next year. The organization responds by creating a highly successful marketing campaign that carries butter sales to all-time highs.

Land O'Lakes introduces Calf Milk Replacer, a revolutionary animal feed that substitutes for the increasingly valuable skim milk that dairy farmers had formerly given their calves.

| 19**52** | 19**53** | 19**57** | 19**58** |

Bridgeman Creameries, a prominent Midwestern maker of ice cream and retailer of milk that had begun its operations in 1882, becomes part of Land O'Lakes. This is Land O'Lakes first acquisition of another business, and for the next three decades the organization operates Bridgeman soda fountains and restaurants.

After the death of longtime President and General Manager John Brandt, the Board of Directors picks Frank Stone as his successor. Previously Land O'Lakes director of sales, Stone will lead the organization for the next 14 years.

The co-op creamery in Mountain Lake, Minn., dissolves to enable members to become direct patrons of Land O'Lakes new multi-purpose dairy plant there. This marks the beginning of a tremendous period of consolidation.

The phasing out of milk cans and the widespread adoption of bulk tanks by Midwestern dairy producers allows Land O'Lakes, for the first time, to procure 100 percent of its Grade A milk from producers with bulk setups.

ALL THE FRESH
Sweet Cream
FROM
11 Quarts of Milk
CHURNED TO MAKE ONE POUND

Quite a handful

Like the housewife in this late-'40s advertisement for Land O'Lakes butter, the organization had its arms full in the post-war years — with technological changes, changing markets, and the formidable competition of margarine.

1947—1962

The Second World War brought about tremendous changes that spurred Land O'Lakes efforts to broaden its vision and diversify its product mix even further. A new generation of consumers had grown up in an era in which butter was a scarce and costly luxury. At the same time, worker shortages had given a boost to grocery stores that featured open shelves from which customers could actually select their purchases without the assistance of a clerk — eventually banishing from markets most bulk, grocer-served products. Any food producer with an eye toward the future had to consider these changes in planning its product lines, packaging and marketing in order to be successful.

It took several years for butter to recover from its wartime slump. Sales of Land O'Lakes Sweet Cream Butter plunged 57 percent between 1940 and 1946, and the nationwide per-capita consumption of butter dropped from 17 pounds to less than 11. But starting in 1946, aggressive marketing at Land O'Lakes and a continued emphasis on producing high-quality butter made their difference, and by 1948, even as other butter manufacturers struggled to make sales, Land O'Lakes butter returned to its pre-war level of popularity — and the company attained its first year of $100 million in sales. It was clear, though, that diversification was the key to survival. Margarine (or "oleo," as it was then called) had made huge gains during the war. When the Margarine Act of 1950 repealed federal laws prohibiting manufacturers from coloring margarine yellow, Land O'Lakes President John Brandt protested, "Let 'em have brown, red, purple, pink, green or any other color, but we had yellow first." But this battle could not be won, and the appearance of yellow margarine in 1951 made it clear that Land O'Lakes had to continue developing new products.

Fortunately, Land O'Lakes had grown into the world's largest producer of dried milk during the war, and it utilized its expertise in milk drying to the fullest in many of its new products. Producing new prod-

Not a dry subject

Dry milk, which Land O'Lakes produced in large quantities during World War II to meet the demands of the armed forces, became the basis of several new products in the 1940s and '50s.

Just add water

By 1951, Land O'Lakes had made inroads in the sale of dry milk to consumers. In-store demonstrators and signs promised that customers could "make milk at home for 7 cents a quart."

ucts from dried milk became the focus of intensive research. Out of that work came instant dried milk for the consumer market, a groundbreaking line of animal feeds, and even a short-lived variety of instant ice cream reconstituted with water. People around the world began seeing the Land O'Lakes name on containers of powdered milk, too. In 1947, after employee Helen Davidson placed her photo and address in a can of dried milk produced for the U.S. government, she was surprised to receive a letter from a woman in Frankfurt, West Germany: "We received a government allotment of powdered milk for Christmas where by accident we came across your picture and address. We can assure you that this powdered milk has been very refreshing. Our wish is that we will receive another like it soon."

The results of the rest of Land O'Lakes diversification drive also were impressive. By 1952, the production of dry milk was up 17-fold from ten years earlier; feed, seed, and fertilizer were up 12-fold; ice cream was up 20-fold; and agronomy sales up six-fold. When John Brandt died in 1953 it certainly spelled the end of an era, but Land O'Lakes and its members were well-placed to reap the benefits of the organization's drive to profit from research, technology and diversification.

One of the more unusual applications of new technology in the post-war years was an automated system for the sale of fluid milk. Some people at Land O'Lakes called it "Maisy, the Mechanical Cow"; others called it the "milk automat." However people referred to it, this unique vending machine, that stood seven feet tall and could dispense more than 200 half-gallons of milk a day, symbolized Land O'Lakes exploration of new ideas. Starting in 1952, Land O'Lakes put 29 "Maisy" machines into service at gas stations, supermarkets, university housing projects, and other sites in the Twin Cities and southern Minnesota. The fluid milk that people bought from the vending machines was a new Land O'Lakes product — a 50,000-quarts-per-day business that kept four bottling plants busy in Minnesota and Wisconsin. The machines themselves were just one more example of some serious thinking at Land O'Lakes about how to take advantage of America's newest food buying trend: self-service. Maisy allowed customers to serve themselves 24 hours a day, with the milk priced four cents a half-gallon less than in stores.

LAND O'LAKES
CREAMERIES INCORPORATED

GENERAL OFFICES
MINNEAPOLIS, 13, MINNESOTA

July 30, 1947

★ MADE FROM SWEET (*not sour*) CREAM

★ DIRECT *from the* PRODUCER

★ NATIONALLY KNOWN *and* ADVERTISED

THE LARGEST MANUFACTURERS OF SWEET CREAM BUTTER IN THE WORLD

LAND O'LAKES CREAMERIES, Inc.

By *Mary Nicholson*

Buy it by the can or pouch

The organization packaged its dry
milk in a number of ways for
consumers, including in cans and
single-quart pouches.

Buy LAND O'LAKES
nonfat DRY MILK solids in 2 sizes...
save money on both!

*For extra economy,
get the 1 lb. package*
MAKES 5 QUARTS
Save more money with the
large size—the round package
with the convenient snap-top lid.

Handy 6.4 oz. carton
MAKES 2 QUARTS
Each carton contains two sealed
foil packages. Contents of each package
makes one quart of nonfat milk when
mixed with water.

*Fresh, sweet milk with just the fat and
water removed. A product of the world's richest
dairyland, the famous LAND O'LAKES.*

Manufactured by
Land O'Lakes Creameries, Inc., Minneapolis 13, Minn., U.S.A.
2122

**Stationery from the era bears the
colorful Land O'Lakes trademark**

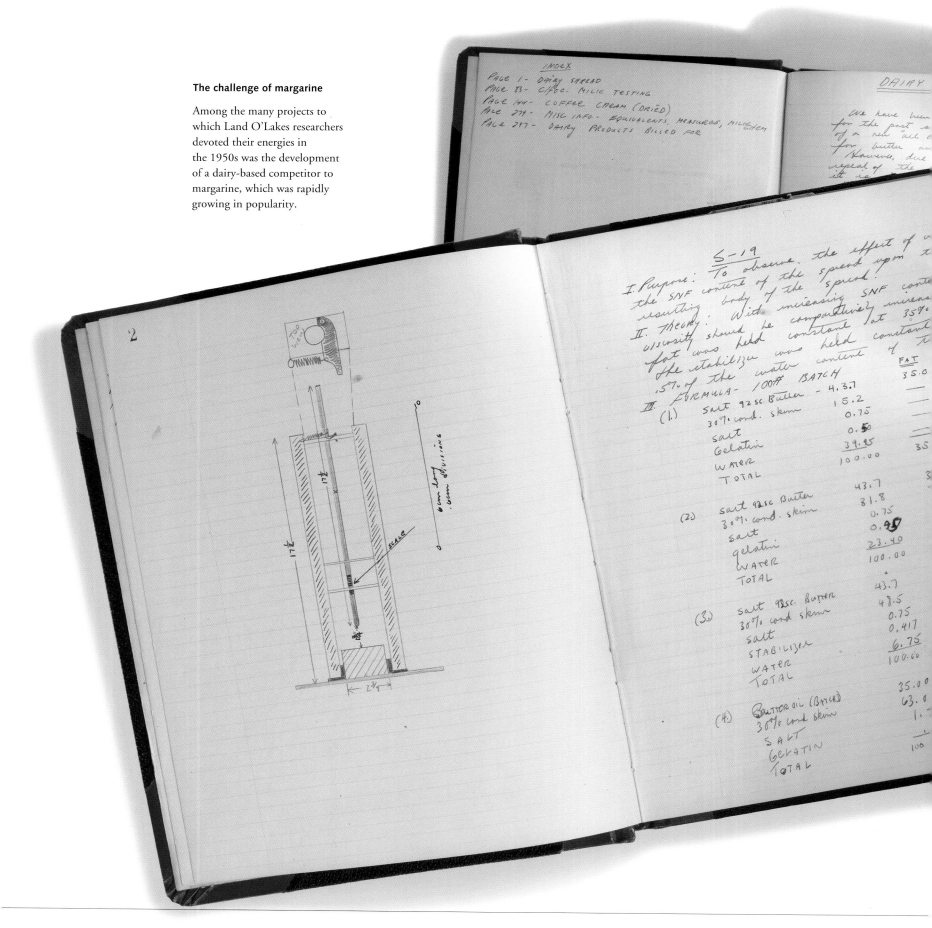

The challenge of margarine

Among the many projects to which Land O'Lakes researchers devoted their energies in the 1950s was the development of a dairy-based competitor to margarine, which was rapidly growing in popularity.

Cool desserts

Land O'Lakes researchers test a new variety of ice cream (above) and an instant ice cream made from powdered milk.

RESEARCHING NEW FOODS

The Land O'Lakes Foods Research department reached many milestones during the post-war years. In 1946, it put onto the road the Midwest's first mobile dairy lab, which toured Land O'Lakes creameries to make tests. "First it will serve as a trouble-shooter in any creamery where the operator needs help in locating the cause of a sag in the quality of his product," said Ben Zakariasen, manager of the Land O'Lakes laboratories. "Second, it will serve as 'insurance' to maintain high quality where no troubles have been encountered."

At Land O'Lakes Minneapolis headquarters, the laboratory facilities included an entire dairy plant in miniature, complete with butter churn, cheese vat, vacuum pan, flash pasteurizer and other up-to-date equipment. In addition to discovering new uses for dry milk solids — one invention was an ice cream mix made from powdered milk — researchers investigated ways to increase the shelf life of products and tested various types of product packaging. Eighty-seven different kinds of packaging for dry milk were tested, for instance, before Land O'Lakes found the right one for the roll-out of the product to grocery stores.

Land O'Lakes home economists created recipes and found new uses for dry milk using a variety of tools that ranged from home kitchen utensils to viscosity meters and Bunsen burners. The staff also fielded inquiries from consumers, who wondered about such things as the cause of "pink butter" (leaking refrigerants in the home ice box were the culprit) and why stuffing a turkey before freezing it often caused spoilage.

Modern labs

Land O'Lakes was justifiably proud of the quality of its labs and lab personnel in the post-war years.

FRANK CRANE:
AN EDISON IN THE FEEDS LAB

Rolling out Calf Milk Replacer

Dr. Frank Crane explains the benefits of Calf Milk Replacer to colleagues.

When Frank Crane arrived at the Land O'Lakes Feed department as a researcher in early 1951, he brought with him little more than a freshly earned doctorate in animal nutrition from the University of Minnesota and the desire to make a mark in the booming animal feed industry. Thirty years later at his retirement, he ranked among the world's most influential and prolific researchers in the field.

"We recognized a real need for a baby calf formula to substitute for milk," Crane recalls. "Farmers were feeding their calves skim milk and gruels, neither of which worked particularly well. What they needed was a more scientifically based formula." The result was Land O'Lakes Calf Milk Replacer, a revolutionary product that farmers could reconstitute simply by adding water. "When working with farm animals, we had to develop products that performed and rewarded farmers economically," Crane says, noting that Land

O'Lakes researchers would extensively test new products at an experimental working farm in Anoka, Minn. "It was important for us to be able to tell farmers what results they could expect from our products. With Calf Milk Replacer, farmers found it performed exactly the way we said it would."

Land O'Lakes vigorously backed Crane's research. "While we didn't have an unlimited budget," he says, "there was great encouragement from the management team for us to pursue our work."

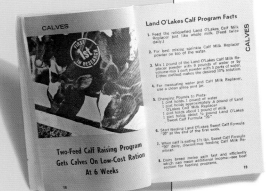

For healthy calves

Land O'Lakes introduced Calf Milk Replacer as part of a complete feeding program for calves.

Better than milk

Among the benefits of Calf Milk
Replacer that Land O'Lakes
promoted to farmers were a much
lower cost than skim milk,
a complete and tested nutritional
formula, and faster growing
calves.

Improved seed varieties also were part of the Ag Services expansion of the '50s

Ag Services grows steadily

The growth of its Ag Services departments contributed much to Land O'Lakes diversification in the 1950s and '60s. Following the introduction of Calf Milk Replacer came a greater variety of feeds for cows, pigs, poultry, sheep and other animals.

The Ag Services solution

As smaller co-op creameries found they could not compete with larger dairy operations in the 1950s and '60s, many — bolstered by Land O'Lakes expanding line of Ag Services products — remained in business by transforming themselves into agricultural supply cooperatives.

Diversified farms

On the diversified farm of the 1950s, dairy production often took place alongside crop and other types of livestock production.

More sanitary procedures

Bulk tank systems made it possible for milk to travel from a cow to a dairy plant without ever coming into contact with contaminants.

Bulk shipping

The tank truck was a sign of the quiet revolution taking place on dairy farms in the 1950s: the introduction of bulk milk tanks to replace the venerable old ten-gallon milk cans. Bulk tanks received milk directly from the farmer's milking machines and kept the fluid refrigerated and away from potential contaminants until pick up by a bulk truck.

From bottles to cartons

As self-service grocery stores became more common throughout the country, Land O'Lakes creameries improved the packaging of their milk containers. Glass bottles were succeeded by cardboard cartons, which were lighter, disposable and easier to arrange in store refrigerator cases.

AL STOMMES:
WITNESS TO MAJOR CHANGE

Few people know the creamery business as well as Al Stommes. Stommes, who's now retired and lives in Cold Spring, Minn., worked for more than 30 years at several co-op creameries in central Minnesota and at a number of Land O'Lakes plants. He witnessed a nearly complete transformation of the dairy manufacturing business during the '50s and '60s largely due to new technology.

"There were only about four people working at the Cold Spring creamery when I started there in 1946," Stommes recalls. "Farmers brought their skimmed cream to the creamery, not their whole milk, because the creamery didn't have a separator at that time." After leaving his creamery job for a stint at the University of Minnesota's ag school, Stommes returned to Cold Spring to serve as creamery manager. "Back then, as manager, you had to do just about everything," he says. "I had to have a 'B' stationary engineering license

to operate the boiler and a butter-making license to operate the churn."

The winds of change began to blow in 1952, when the Cold Spring creamery added separators and began accepting whole milk from farmers. "We'd skim off the cream and make butter from it and then ship the butter off to Land O'Lakes in Minneapolis for printing (packaging)," Stommes says. Then in the early 1960s, continuous churn technology began to be introduced, and a lot of the smaller creameries went out of business. Stommes went on to manage several Land O'Lakes dairy plants, including one in Alexandria, Minn., where he presided over the plant's switchover to continuous churn butter-making equipment.

Indian Maiden: version three

Land O'Lakes butter cartons sold during the 1950s and '60s retained the changes to the carton design made in 1939.

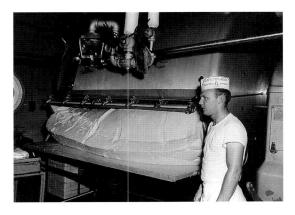

Barrel churns on the wane

The Land O'Lakes dairy plant at Mountain Lake, Minn., was the nation's second butter plant to switch to continuous churn technology.

CREAMERIES IN TRANSITION

The number of local creameries in the country began to decline in the 1950s, but the production levels of the remaining creameries increased. By 1958, butter producing facilities nationwide had fallen in number to 2,062 from the 4,660 in operation twenty years before. Similar declines took place among Land O'Lakes member creameries. Plants that produced cheese, ice cream, and evaporated milk also became less numerous.

A steady consolidation of smaller dairy plants into larger ones was in the making — mainly due to new technology. In 1957 the Mountain Lake, Minn., co-op creamery became the first member creamery to dissolve itself so that its members could become direct patrons of the new Land O'Lakes multi-purpose dairy plant in that community. As technology made larger plants more practical, small local creameries had a tough time competing with larger dairy plants. The smallest butter manufacturers, for instance, spent twice as much to produce a pound of butter as the largest. The use of the continuous churn, a butter-producing process that used large amounts of cream to produce butter in a steady flow instead of in batches, placed further pressure on the creameries that were too small to install the new equipment. In late 1964 Land O'Lakes equipped its dairy plant in Mountain Lake with continuous churn machinery — making it the second plant in the nation to receive such technology.

The Mountain Lake, Minn., plant

M.L. Totten, Land O'Lakes
director of sales during most of
the 1950s

Marketing pros

Land O'Lakes sales managers
meet to discuss new strategies.

MARKETING FOR A NEW AGE

Gone were many of the Mom and Pop grocery stores. TV had pulled ahead of radio, newspapers, and magazines as the top media outlet. And Americans were eating more margarine than butter. Land O'Lakes responded to these important changes in the late 1950s by launching a marketing counter-offensive suited to an age of new eating habits and media strength. Instead of buying newspaper ads, the company signed on Crusader Rabbit, a popular cartoon character, to promote Land O'Lakes ice cream on TV. In-store displays designed for supermarkets pitched Land O'Lakes powdered milk. The largest ad campaign in Land O'Lakes history focused on television, not print, advertising to extoll the purity and wholesomeness of Land O'Lakes butter — implicitly casting the purity and wholesomeness of margarine in doubt.

Even premiums, which Land O'Lakes had used as early as the '30s to help sell butter, acquired a new sophistication. Customers in 1960 could receive their own miniature copper cream can by sending in $1.50 and a butter carton panel — and they did to the tune of $1 million. That marketing gambit sold a lot of butter and reminded customers that there was fresh, sweet cream (not vegetable oil) in the spread they purchased.

A fleet of eighteen-wheelers

Trucks replaced trains as the favored means of shipping Land O'Lakes products long distance by the late '50s.

TAKE ONE GIANT-STEP—*and dream a thousand meadows. Feel the breeze blow fresh. You're in the Land O'Lakes—America's richest dairyland!*

The copper can that could

In 1960, Land O'Lakes began offering miniature copper cream cans as premiums to consumers who sent in $1.50 and a panel from a butter carton. More than $1 million worth of the cans were sold.

Why we use a full ½ gallon of fresh, sweet cream to churn each pound of Land O'Lakes Butter*

HERE IN THE LAND OF LAKES AND MEADOWS, where the good things of life are *so* bountiful, we use only *sweet* cream—a full half gallon—to churn each pound of Land O'Lakes Butter.

Some people, of course, think it a little odd that we make such a fuss over the sweet cream we use (we admit we frequently reject cream that *tastes* sweet simply because it's not sweet *enough* for Land O'Lakes Butter); and we know some find it hard to believe we use a *full half gallon* of this sweet cream to every pound.

But it's true. And we'd no more think of changing it than we'd think of removing the pitchers of cream from our own breakfast tables.

You see, up here, this Land O'Lakes Butter of ours is more than a product; it's a standard of living. For many of us, it's our life work. We stake our reputations on it.

That's why we will not sell a single pound of our Land O'Lakes brand butter that does not meet the highest commercial score any butter can achieve—as graded on official United States Butter Grading Standards.

That's why we will not drop even one—no, not even one—of the 19 separate tests each pound of our butter must pass before it is released for sale.

Maybe it's just our way of life. Up here —where the breeze blows fresh—we set our sights pretty high. And, judging from your response, a lot of you folks must be glad we do.

So we're going to keep right on *insisting* that a *full half gallon* of fresh, sweet cream go into every single pound of Land O'Lakes Butter.

We hope *you* will sort of ins⋯ stock it for you. (Most *qualit⋯*

*LIGHTLY SALTED OR UNSALTED

The success of the Cenex/Land O'Lakes Agronomy Co. is good evidence of the overall success of the Land O'Lakes and Cenex joint venture, which was established in 1987. The Agronomy Co. is owned 50/50 by Land O'Lakes and Cenex, and supplies member cooperatives with plant food and crop protection products, as well as a host of technical services, including AgriSource, a computerized information management system.

"We believe that 'Precision Agriculture' is the wave of the future in agronomics," says Dave Johnson, president of the Agronomy Co. Precision Agriculture refers to the successful management of people, knowledge and technology in a way that results in the efficient and environmentally responsible application of plant food and crop protection products.

Paul Liebenstein is a Land O'Lakes dairy producer from Dundas, Minn. He gets his agronomy products from the Cannon Valley Co-op in Northfield. "Since dairying is our number-one concern and takes up the majority of our time, we rely heavily on the co-op for such things as crop scouting, pest control and recommendations for manure management," Liebenstein says. "The service we get from Cannon Valley is unmatched. Plus, since it's a co-op, we're part owners, and that means the employees work for us. I really like that."

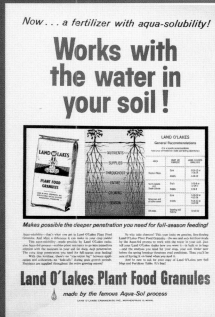

Paul Liebenstein (left), a dairy producer from Dundas, Minn.; and Craig Maurer, agronomy manager, Cannon Valley Co-op

A Land O'Lakes fertilizer ad from 1960

19**63**—19**81**

FROM FARM TO MARKET

19**63**

19**64**

19**69**

As a result of a number of mergers, acquisitions and entries into various ag product lines over the years, Land O'Lakes had grown into a diverse agricultural supply and food marketing co-op by the early 1970s.

Land O'Lakes acquires Dairy Belt Cheese and Butter Company of Spencer, Wis. This purchase allows the organization to enter the cheese market in big way.

Land O'Lakes becomes a member of Central Farmers Fertilizer Company (today known as CF Industries), which allows the organization to offer its members a wide variety of plant foods.

It is an era of numerous acquisitions and mergers for Land O'Lakes, with 37 taking place this year alone.

1970

1972

1980

1981

Land O'Lakes merges with Farmers Regional Cooperative (Felco), based in Fort Dodge, Iowa. The merger marks the beginning of tremendous growth in Ag Services.

Land O'Lakes introduces its first margarine, a high-quality product that has undergone extensive formulation and test marketing.

The 4-Quart cheese line begins appearing in the nation's grocery stores. In time, the line will establish Land O'Lakes as the nation's leading marketer of deli cheese.

Wisconsin's Lake to Lake Dairy Cooperative joins the Land O'Lakes family, bringing 1,342 new member-owners into the organization, as well as a strong consumer cheese presence in California.

LAND O LAKES
FELCO®

Land O'Lakes bounty

This shot from the late 1970s features a full range of products — from feed, seed and spark plugs to cheese, turkey breasts and ice cream novelties — that symbolized the organization's marketing philosophy of bringing agricultural products all the way from the farm to the consumer.

1963—1981

When the bell sounded on August 20, 1971 in the Land O'Lakes butter print room in Minneapolis, workers there switched off the machinery for the last time. After 45 years of continuous production and the packaging of 2.5 billion pounds of butter, the print room was closing. That same year Land O'Lakes sold off its unprofitable Equipment Sales division, and in 1973 a Land O'Lakes milk plant accepted the organization's last shipment of milk in old 10-gallon cans. These endings, though poignant and even painful to some Land O'Lakes members, were signs of a momentous shifting of emphasis in the organization. The 1960s and '70s ushered in an era of do-or-die change. The speed and efficiency of the continuous churn and soft-butter print processes made old-style print rooms obsolete. During the five decades of Equipment Sales division's operation, other sources of equipment sprang up for dairy plants. And beginning in the 1950s, bulk milk tanks had gradually left milk cans quaint relics of the past.

Land O'Lakes discarded the old not haphazardly, but with a new marketing philosophy in mind. Through a series of acquisitions and mergers over many years — Land O'Lakes acquired 37 smaller cooperatives, dairies and agricultural service organizations in 1969 alone — the membership grew much larger and far more diverse. Now Land O'Lakes farmer-members were not only operators of dairy farms, but also growers of soybeans, alfalfa, wheat and corn; and producers of hogs, beef cattle and poultry. The 1970 merger of Land O'Lakes with Felco, a strong agricultural services cooperative headquartered in Fort Dodge, Iowa, increased the number of member-patrons three-fold

Advancements in the kitchen and dairy case

Staff home economist Lois Horsley demonstrates a dry milk-based baking product of the 1960s (right). A promotional store dairy case (far right) shows an idealized display of the full line of Land O'Lakes dairy products.

while vastly improving the organization's expertise and capabilities in feed, seed, and fertilizers. While Land O'Lakes had been in the ag supply business some 40 years prior to its merger with Felco, that business had always been relatively small — accounting for less than 10 percent of total sales annually. With the Felco merger, Ag Service sales jumped to more than 20 percent of Land O'Lakes total business and have grown steadily ever since. On the dairy side of the business, many other organizations — really too many to mention all of them — joined the Land O'Lakes family, including Dairy Belt Cheese and Butter Company, Yegen Dairy Company, Clover Dairy Company, H.C. Christians Company, Dairy Maid, Sanitary Farm Dairies, Dakota Dairies, and Lake to Lake Dairy Cooperative. Finally it was within Land O'Lakes grasp to become a true "farm-to-market" organization, one that could provide farmer-members with the necessary agricultural supplies, production facilities, marketing know-how, and brand-name recognition to deliver virtually their whole output of products and livestock all the way to the end user.

The Dairy Belt acquisition in 1963 gave Land O'Lakes a large and well-equipped cheese-making facility in Spencer, Wis., and this site soon became the center of the organization's production and packaging of bulk, processed, dried, and natural cheeses. Later, the Felco merger sparked a huge expansion of Land O'Lakes Ag Services activities, giving farmer-members of all varieties the materials with which to raise their diversity of crops and livestock. Other changes came with experimental forays into such activities as margarine production and red meat processing. Some of these experiments resulted in permanent additions to the organization's product line (margarine), while others were short-lived (red meat). Regardless of the outcomes, no one could deny that Land O'Lakes was broadening its benefits for members. Nor could anyone deny that these changes kept Land O'Lakes financially strong. Sales, fueled by the Felco merger, soared to $654 million in 1970, and ten years later they had more than doubled from that. Even the old stand-by, butter, continued to pull its weight — in 1974, when Americans consumed nearly three times as much margarine as butter, Land O'Lakes recorded the biggest butter sales in its history and towered above all competitors in butter marketing.

In 1981 the organization's growth and changes in emphasis became visible to the eye with the completion of Land O'Lakes new headquarters, built in Arden Hills, Minn., on a 48-acre wooded site eight miles from its old Minneapolis home.

Boxed to go

A Land O'Lakes cheese package from the era of the company's strong push into cheese production and marketing.

The cheese capital of Land O'Lakes

The Spencer, Wis., cheese plant, which came to Land O'Lakes as part of the acquisition of Dairy Belt Cheese and Butter Company in 1963, became the center of the organization's process cheese production.

JOHN CARR:
MORE THAN FORTY YEARS IN SALES

John Carr became head of Branch Sales at Land O'Lakes in 1964. At the time, Land O'Lakes food sales and distribution were handled through 23 branch offices, most of which were located in cities in the eastern half of the United States. Each of the branch offices was responsible for its own profitability, and in many ways they behaved like independent companies. It was a system that, by the time he came to oversee it, Carr knew extremely well.

Carr had begun his career at Land O'Lakes in 1933 as a warehouseman in Philadelphia — turning down a competing offer by Connie Mack to play baseball for the Athletics. He rose through the ranks at Land O'Lakes, as did many of his generation, eventually becoming a salesman, and later branch manager in Baltimore, New York and Chicago. "Land O'Lakes was truly like a family back then," says Larry Hokanson, who worked

for Carr as a regional sales manager. "Co-workers socialized with each other much more in those days, took fishing trips with each other, and knew more about each others' lives and families," he says. "Although Carr could be a tough taskmaster," Hokanson concludes, "he was probably the fairest man I have ever met." Among Carr's lasting legacies to Land O'Lakes was opening up the sales force to women in 1975.

Packing the goods

Employees at the Spencer, Wis., cheese plant pack and prepare cheese for shipment.

Part of Land O'Lakes growing line of cheese products

"Imagine! Margarine from America's No. 1 butter maker."

It takes a butter company to give your customers the taste they really want in a margarine.

The quality reputation of Land O'Lakes butter became a selling point in the promotion of margarine

Bearing the label

In order to bear the Land O'Lakes label, the organization determined that the new margarine product had to be of the highest quality.

A LAND O'LAKES MARGARINE

After decades of deriding margarine as a fraudulent product masquerading as butter, and pressing for laws that made it unlawful for manufacturers to color margarine yellow, Land O'Lakes itself became a margarine producer and marketer in the 1970s. Several events sparked Land O'Lakes entry into the margarine market. One was the merger with Felco, which brought into the Land O'Lakes fold thousands of soybean and corn farmers needing markets for vegetable oil. Another was a shift in the organization's thinking: "We began to see that butter was butter and margarine was margarine, and that we should be in the spreads business, not just the butter business," explains Harvey Ebert, a Land O'Lakes vice president at the time. Finally, the organization acknowledged that margarine, by giving Land O'Lakes a more complete spreads line for grocery dairy cases and institutional users, could help ensure the continuance of a market for Land O'Lakes dairy-based products. Land O'Lakes margarine first appeared in 1972, after the testing of a dozen different formulations and scores of styles of packaging. The product rolled out gradually to different geographic markets. At last in 1976, the organization's first margarine-dedicated plant opened in Hudson, Iowa, and the "margarine from America's No. 1 butter maker" became fully established in Land O'Lakes product array.

King of the road

As the production volume of Land O'Lakes plants increased, the tanker trucks got longer and longer.

LAND O'LAKES AND FELCO

In 1969, Land O'Lakes began merger discussions with Iowa-based Farmers Regional Cooperative (Felco), an organization itself the product of merged agricultural cooperatives whose origins stretched all the way back to 1921. The Batelle Memorial Research Institute, an independent consulting facility, recommended that merger be seriously explored, explaining that even though both Land O'Lakes and Felco were "strong, financially sound, well managed, profitable, [and] viable farmer-cooperatives," together they could strengthen their efforts serving farmer-members.

Felco had long specialized in agricultural "inputs" (farm supplies), while marketing some soy products, and Land O'Lakes had focused on "outputs" (dairy products), while selling some feed, seed, and fertilizers. The merger, when it occurred in 1970 with the overwhelming approval of members, instantly transformed the new Land O'Lakes, Inc. (renamed from Land O'Lakes Creameries, Inc.) into a much more diversified organization with 10,000 member patrons and $654 million in sales. Felco's headquarters in Fort Dodge, Iowa, became the center of the new organization's Ag Services operation. With this strong combination of facilities and talents, a new Land O'Lakes was born.

So long, Maiden

The Land O'Lakes/Felco merger ended the appearance of the Indian Maiden logo on Ag Services product packaging — except for milk replacers.

Land O'Lakes Iowa home base

Felco's Fort Dodge headquarters became the center of Land O'Lakes Ag Services activities after the merger.

The new team

Shortly after the merger with Felco, the management staff of Land O'Lakes gathered for a photograph. They included (from left) Richard Magnuson, V.P. and General Counsel; Rolf Haugen, V.P. of Finance; Philip Stocker, V.P. of General Services; Ralph Hofstad, Senior V.P. of Agricultural Services; Dave Henry, President; Harvey Ebert, Senior V.P. Food Processing and Marketing; Don Renquist, V.P. Personnel; Gerald Matlin, V.P. Information Systems; and Vern Moore, V.P. Administration and Corporate Planning.

Sign of the times

A new Ag Services logo reflected the identity of both Land O'Lakes and Felco.

How to help more arrive, survive and thrive.

RALPH HOFSTAD:
A CO-OP VISIONARY AND OPTIMIST

In 1965, when Ralph Hofstad went to Felco to head up the Iowa ag services cooperative after 17 years with a co-op organization in Illinois, little did he realize that before the decade was over, he would preside over Felco's merger with Land O'Lakes. But within a short time of his arrival at Felco, Hofstad saw that the organization had to broaden its activities. "The farmer was telling us, 'You've helped us on the farm, but who's going to help us get better prices in the marketplace?'" he recalls. A consultant identified Land O'Lakes as a cooperative whose marketing strengths nicely complemented Felco's ag service muscle, and a merger took effect in 1970.

Hofstad became senior vice president of Land O'Lakes expanded Ag Services division. "There was an element of risk assimilating the two different cultures,"he says. "But it worked out because Felco and Land O'Lakes had a common mission to serve farmers." Four years later, Hofstad began his 15-year term as president of Land O'Lakes. He expanded the organization's marketing efforts and built up its strengths in both Dairy Foods and Ag Services. "A cooperative is different from a regular corporation — it has to respond to the needs of its members," he says. "I've always been a visionary and an optimist, someone willing to take risks. If you take the right risks, the rewards can be tremendous."

A litter of new ads

The strength of the Land O'Lakes/Felco Ag Services operations came through in a series of new ads promoting feed, seeds, and agronomy products.

An editorial merger

The merger of Land O'Lakes and Felco took place editorially with the creation of a new organizational magazine — the *Land O'Lakes Mirror*, which replaced the *Land O'Lakes News* and the *Felco Mirror*.

LAND O LAKES

LAND O'LAKES, INC., AGRICULTURAL SERVICES
2827 8TH AVENUE SOUTH • PHONE (515) 576-7311
FORT DODGE, IOWA 50501

LAND O LAKES
FELCO
AGRICULTURAL SERVICES

LAND O LAKES
QUALITY FOODS

July 31, 1973

FOR IMMEDIATE RELEASE

Site grading for building construction is underway on the new 535 acre Land O'Lakes, Inc. research farm located ten miles east of Fort Dodge, Iowa. By early 1974, eleven buildings will have been completed at the research farm where LAND O LAKES-FELCO branded products will be tested. The farm will formally be open for public tours next summer at the Farm-O-Rama Days scheduled in August.

The new research facility consolidates operations that have been carried out on two smaller farms—one five miles east of Fort Dodge and the other near Hampton, Minnesota, southeast of the Twin Cities.

The new Land O'Lakes farm will include both livestock and agronomy research. In the livestock area, work will be done with swine, turkeys, beef feeding, beef cow-calf and animal milk products. Agronomy work will include soybean and forage breeding, pasture mixes and fertilization, and chemical and fertilizer research and demonstration. Demonstration results are tied closely to Land O'Lakes' marketing effort.

The turkey and beef cow-calf research projects will be part of Cooperative Research Farms, a national research organization involving Land O'Lakes, Inc. and twenty other regional coopera- tives. Land O'Lakes has been a part of the Cooperative Research Farms program since 1959.

Another important aspect of the new Land O'Lakes farm is pollution control research in animal wastes, chemicals and fertilizers. Ways of handling, storing and using these animal wastes will be studied to determine which are most feasible for the farmer.

Three swine buildings will be constructed on the farm. They will be utilized primarily as

A farm with the answers

It was with great pride that Land O'Lakes unveiled its new agricultural research facility, the Answer Farm, in 1974. Located near the Land O'Lakes Fort Dodge Ag Services headquarters, the farm was a testing site for new products. It drew 30,000 visitors — many of them farmer-members — in its first three years.

Scientist at work

Dr. Drew Ivers, director of plant research, specialized in the development of new soybean varieties.

Cash crops

Two new varieties of alfalfa were typical of the seed products offered by Land O'Lakes/Felco.

A full line of Ag Service products

Ag Services at Land O'Lakes became more of an equal partner with the dairy portion of the business after the Land O'Lakes and Felco merger, meeting the needs of farmer-members who raised a variety of crops and livestock.

The Vincent, Iowa, seed plant

A source of information

In addition to products, Land O'Lakes also provided information on good animal management practices.

A beef feed lot on the Great Plains

More varieties of species

Dairy cows, once the most important animal at Land O'Lakes, were forced to surrender their domination of the organization's attention once the Felco merger brought more producers of hogs, sheep, beef cattle, and other species into the Land O'Lakes family in the 1970s.

Land O'Lakes President Ralph Hofstad (left) and Board Chairman Melvin Sprecher (right) met with Kansas Senator Bob Dole when the board visited Washington, D.C., in 1976

The new Land O'Lakes headquarters in Arden Hills, Minn., opened in 1981

A NEW FOCUS ON DAIRY

The early 1980s were an exciting time for Land O'Lakes. Much of the previous decade had been dominated by the merger with Felco and the subsequent transformation of a largely dairy-oriented Land O'Lakes into an organization that was substantially more agriculturally diverse. The beginning of the '80s, however, saw attention again swing back toward dairy with the merger in 1981 of Land O'Lakes and Lake to Lake, a well-respected eastern Wisconsin dairy cooperative that specialized in natural cheese.

Land O'Lakes also experimented with a number of innovative new food products in the early '80s. One of the most imaginative was Country Morning Blend, which was the first of a number of lighter spreads Land O'Lakes began to develop. When Land O'Lakes introduced Country Morning Blend in 1981, the price of butter was significantly higher than the price of margarine. "A lot of people wanted to buy butter, but felt they couldn't because of the price," explains Peggy Ellingson, a veteran Land O'Lakes spreads marketer. "We believed there was a need for a product that was in between the two." First appearing in a formulation of 40 percent butter and 60 percent corn-oil margarine, its sales slogan, "Tastes like butter because it's made with butter," said it all.

Land O'Lakes welcomes Lake to Lake

In 1981, Lake to Lake Dairy Cooperative, a strong marketer of cheese and non-fat dry milk, merged with Land O'Lakes. It brought along its 1,342 dairy producers, a well-known branded cheese business with good market share in California, and 35 years of dairy experience in eastern Wisconsin.

The best of both worlds

Country Morning Blend
promised consumers the taste of
butter at a fraction of
the cost, and it delivered. The
product was a 40 percent
butter, 60 percent margarine mix.

New Country Morning Blend combines 40%
Land O Lakes sweet cream butter with pure
corn oil. What you get is corn oil's natural light-
ness with butter's delicious taste. At less cost
than butter. Country Morning Blend. It's a better
idea. Better yet, it's a butter idea. Tastes like
butter, because it's made with butter. Country
Morning Blend. New from Land O' Lakes.

Lightly salted and sweet unsalted.

Country Morning Blend from LAND O LAKES®

Land O'Lakes signed one of its first foreign contracts for the sale of butter with an importer in Lima, Peru, in 1925. Although Land O'Lakes continued to market such products as powdered milk and calf milk replacer overseas through the 1970s, it was with the establishment of an International Development division in 1981 that the cooperative's overseas activities became truly focused.

Today, Land O'Lakes is involved in overseas training and development, as well as in the manufacture and sale of proprietary products. The International Development division focuses on assisting private sector cooperatives and agribusinesses in developing nations, while the International Marketing group is involved in the sale and manufacture of both feed and food products in several countries around the world.

One of the countries where Land O'Lakes has a growing presence is Poland. Land O'Lakes is involved in a feed manufacturing project there, as well as a cheese-making venture. Peter Banaszak is feed sales manager for Land O'Lakes Agra in Miescisko, Poland. "It's exciting to be on the leading edge of industry development in Poland," Banaszak says. "Selling high-quality feed is very rewarding work for me because I am well acquainted with the poor quality products that were available in the past."

Peter Banaszak (left), Land O'Lakes feed sales manager, Miescisko, Poland; and Bogdan Malengowski, a Miescisko-area farmer

A Spanish-labeled can of powdered milk, circa 1950

1982—1996

ONE OF THE BEST

A new spirit of cooperation

In response to local cooperative leaders, the Land O'Lakes and Cenex boards of directors have reached agreement to consolidate their farm supply operations in joint ventures to better serve farmers. Facts about this innovative plan, which will be considered by local cooperative directors in November, are presented in the following pages.

19**82**	19**87**	19**91**

The skills and dedication of thousands of cooperative members and employees, some of whom are pictured here, are helping to make Land O'Lakes one of the best food and agricultural companies in the world.

Land O'Lakes merges with Midland Cooperatives, a Minneapolis-based ag supply co-op with sales of $511 million that brings strength in feed, seed, agronomy and petroleum to the organization.

An innovative joint venture with Cenex results in shared ownership of the Cenex/Land O'Lakes Agronomy Co. and a marketing effort that unifies the Feed and Seed operations owned by Land O'Lakes with the Petroleum operations owned by Cenex.

Foodservice cheese volume at Land O'Lakes exceeds 100 million pounds a year for the first time, growing 4 percent annually — three times the industry average.

1991

1992

1993

1996

Land O'Lakes International Development activities grow to involve more than 200 training courses and outreach programs attracting participants from 32 different countries.

No•Fat Sour Cream, a new no-fat product for the consumer market, is introduced. It has the great taste of regular sour cream, and soon is the number-one seller in its category nationwide.

The Western Feed division, which is responsible for expansion of Land O'Lakes feed sales in the Pacific Northwest, itself expands to Hawaii and all the way west to Guam.

At its 75th Annual Meeting in February, Land O'Lakes celebrates its best year ever, with earnings in each of its core businesses — Feed, Seed, Agronomy, and Dairy Foods — exceeding plan.

Proud and strong

The Farmers Cooperative Company of Aurelia, Iowa, proudly displays the new Ag Service logo developed after the merger with Midland Cooperatives in 1982.

1982—1996

The fact that it happened in an era known more for its risky leveraged buy-outs and hostile take-overs made it truly an unusual marriage of organizations. In 1986 Land O'Lakes announced that it had reached an agreement to combine forces with Cenex, a 56-year-old regional cooperative based in St. Paul — and the agreement involved neither a buy-out nor a merger. Instead, the two cooperatives simply decided to operate their Ag Service divisions as joint ventures, with each organization retaining its own independence and individuality. This ground-breaking arrangement came five years after the Land O'Lakes merger with Midland Cooperatives, which strengthened Land O'Lakes ag supply business in the Upper Midwest. It was the result of a growing realization at Land O'Lakes that new approaches to doing business would be needed in order to respond to the accelerating changes of the late 20th century.

"This joint venture proposal is indicative of what cooperatives should be best at — cooperation," said Land O'Lakes Board Chairman Claire Sandness, at the time the agreement was reached. "The driving force behind this joint venture was information we obtained from our members. They wanted us to do what we could to make the cooperative system more economically competitive and eliminate the extra programs, facilities and services that exist. We feel this joint venture is an important step in that direction."

The nationwide farm crisis, which began in the early 1980s with a devastating combination of weak commodity markets, rising production costs and high interest rates, spotlighted the urgent needs of producers. The old patterns of relatively stable prices and a predictable income based on tried and true methods were disintegrating. So Land O'Lakes established simple yet tough goals: to eliminate wasteful duplication, develop its exist-

A good fit

Land O'Lakes merger with Midland Cooperatives in 1982 brought together two organizations with common goals, similar ag product lines and supply sources.

Tough times

During the farm crisis of the early 1980s, those producers who could keep working their land faced exceptionally low commodity prices.

ing businesses, kindle new ones, strive to be least-cost, and, above all, focus on its customers — all with the aim of keeping producers and local cooperatives competitive in a changing international marketplace. The Land O'Lakes which emerged from that era is proving to be financially strong and intensely focused on ensuring that local cooperatives and producer-members will be able to benefit from the technological and marketing advances of the future. Feed, Seed, Agronomy and Dairy Foods have blossomed, in part, because of Land O'Lakes commitment to learning and investment in people in its quest to become one of the best food and agricultural companies in the world.

Far from the fields and communities of Land O'Lakes members, a huge international market awaits tapping, and Land O'Lakes is working to bring that market closer to members, too. In 1981 the organization formally established an International division. Since then, among its many international projects, Land O'Lakes has focused on building new business in Eastern Europe and has launched the manufacturing and sale of feed and cheese products in Poland.

Land O'Lakes has not let slip its longstanding ability to develop new dairy-based products for the domestic market, either: No•Fat and Light Sour Cream, Light Butter, and Spread with Sweet Cream all rolled onto the market during the 1980s and '90s. Land O'Lakes remains unique among U.S. dairy cooperatives in its ability to successfully leverage its widely known brand name and create value-added consumer products, which include the nation's number-one line of deli cheese. Foodservice and Custom Products businesses also have attained record sales gains at Land O'Lakes in recent years, and the organization's flagship product, Land O'Lakes Sweet Cream Butter, remains America's only nationally distributed butter — commanding a 31 percent share of the retail market.

Land O'Lakes can remain only as strong as the communities in which its members and employees live and work. So, during the 1990s, Land O'Lakes committed itself to invest 2 percent of its pretax earnings each year in helping to improve the quality of life and the well-being of its member communities and rural areas. Most of these contributions go to non-profit organizations that combat hunger in rural America, and much of the rest helps fund leadership programs for rural youth. Land O'Lakes works to further leverage these funds by encouraging volunteerism on the part of its employees and retirees.

A new symbol for the Farm-To-Food System

Land O'Lakes merger with Midland Cooperatives in 1982 strengthened all the Ag Service divisions of the new organization. Land O'Lakes relationship with farmers was enhanced as a result of its new partnership with hundreds of Midland-affiliated member co-ops. A fresh symbol was developed to represent this new "Farm-To-Food" System, and soon it began appearing on trucks, feed and seed bags, fertilizer spreaders, propane tanks and service stations throughout the Upper Midwest.

Where The Farm-To-Food System Begins

It's there — watching over America — from the farm to the city ... from the field to the table. It's the source of America's greatness. Allowing Americans to go about the business of industry, science and technology with no fears about the quality or quantity of foods available. It's the beginning of The Farm-to-Food System.

You, the American farmer, are the cornerstone. Helping to build The Farm-to-Food System into the most efficient, most productive, most dependable System in the world.

Your local cooperative plays an important role in The System, too. Providing needed production inputs such as feed, fertilizer, fuel and a stable market for farm commodities.

Land O'Lakes also works beside You and Your Cooperative in The System bringing together a national network of research, manufacturing and distribution capabilities to provide You with a reliable flow of high-quality products, services and technology.

Side by side, You, Your Cooperative and Land O'Lakes hold the key to abundant foodstuff production ... the source of the prosperity that has made America's Farm-to-Food System the envy of the world, the foundation of a glorious past and the blueprint for an exciting future.

TM-Trademark of Land O'Lakes, Inc.

You, Your Cooperative and Land O'Lakes
Where The Farm-To-Food System Begins

Processor of the year

In 1984 and 1989 *Dairy Record* honored Land O'Lakes as its Processor of the Year.

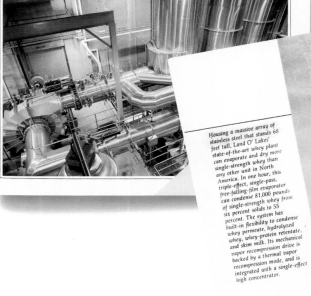

A Gorman Publication

DAIRY RECORD

Vol. 85, No. 12   Incorporating American Dairy Review   December 1984

PROCESSOR OF THE YEAR
LAND O' LAKES
- How an R&D commitment has molded a market leader
- Brand-name power in consumer and foodservice markets
- Sharpening the edge with state-of-the-art plants
—page 58

FOOD TECHNOLOGY
- Making whey a marketable ingredient —page 86

New West Coast firm hails flan as yogurt's successor
Sacramento, Calif.—A European food firm, backed by Spanish and American investors, has set up a new company here to manufacture and market fresh, milk-based flan. According to The American Dhul Corporation, the U.S. market is ready for refrigerated, ready-to-eat desserts. *Story on page 16.*

Snapple Juice taps health trend with Vitamin Supreme
Ridgewood, N.J.—With the demand for more healthful beverages gaining momentum, Snapple Juice Company may have come up with the "ultimate juice." Snapple expects its new vitamin-boosted juice to keep the company on its phenomenal growth pattern. *Story on page 30.*

Fromageries Bel's crazy campaign increases sales 50 percent
Hoboken, N.J.—When Fromageries Bel, maker of Laughing Cow cheeses, decided to launch its first consumer ad campaign, the company came up with off-beat radio spots that have boosted sales in New York City. *Story on page 24.*

MIF/IAICM begin push for market-oriented support program
San Francisco—At their annual meeting, the MIF and IAICM boards approved farm-bill recommendations to end production-management programs to reduce government purchases. Instead, they favor adjustments in the support price to reflect market conditions. *Story on page 51.*

Land O' Lakes: The market-driven co-op

Housing a massive array of stainless steel that stands 68 feet tall, Land O' Lakes' state-of-the-art whey plant can evaporate and dry more single-strength whey than any other unit in North America. In one hour, this triple-effect, single-pass, free-falling-film evaporator can condense 81,000 pounds of single-strength whey from six percent solids to 55 percent. The system has built-in flexibility to condense whey permeate, hydrolyzed whey, whey-protein retentate, and skim milk. Its mechanical vapor recompression drive is backed by a thermal vapor recompression mode, and is integrated with a single-effect high concentrator.

Photos by John Krupka.

Processor of the Year
LAND O' LAKES

Kiel, Wisconsin
What a Good Merger Can Bring

A showcase cheese plant also becomes a showcase whey powdering plant

By Clem Honer

The 1981 merger between Lake to Lake and Land O' Lakes has proven to be one of the most mutually beneficial mergers in dairy history. While there were many factors that made the marriage so successful, each co-op brought something special to the relationship. For Land O' Lakes, it was an ever-growing power in both marketing and R&D; for Lake to Lake, it was—among other things—a commitment to state-of-the art designing and building.

Today, the Lake to Lake division plant at Kiel, Wisconsin, stands as a working monument to that merger. Kiel is the home of one of the finest cheddar cheese plants in the U.S.— a Lake to Lake plant built prior to the merger that remains a showplace of advanced design, state-of-the-art engineering, and outstanding product quality. In a co-op family that claims more than 30 dairy plants, including some eight cheese plants, Kiel is arguably the most advanced.

Among the plant's distinctions is that it produced the 1984 World Cheese Award winner. This year's competition included 542 entries from 14 countries.

What makes the Kiel complex even more remarkable today is a new, $7.5-million whey powdering plant that came on stream this fall. Cost-justified by Land O' Lakes' mushrooming success in marketing whey, the plant is a showcase facility in the best Lake to Lake tradition. It is designed to dry non-hydroscopic whole-whey powder,

[text continues off page: various fractions of whey, and skim... The evaporator... capable of p... per hour tha... combination... according t... to Lake's d... The equ... building t... and conta... floor spac... occupy 10... product s... feet—en... nine ful... At fu... can con... from s... cent s... pound... ultrafi... six pe... rate... hydr... to 6... pou... whe... per... ho... ed... of...]

Ads tell the story

Dairy Foods advertising from
the 1980s and '90s shows
the expansion of Land O'Lakes
line of dairy-based products.

DIVERSIFICATION IN DAIRY FOODS

If by the 1980s any consumers, foodservice organizations or food processors still thought of Land O'Lakes as just a butter company, the introduction of a host of innovative dairy products during the decade certainly should have changed their minds. In addition to adding a variety of margarines and butter-margarine blends to its spreads line, Land O'Lakes rolled out to the foodservice industry Sour Creme Supreme, a fresh-tasting sour cream with a three-month shelf life. Lean Cream, an early low-fat product now known to consumers as Light Sour Cream, made a big splash in the retail market shortly thereafter. It quickly rose to number-one market share in its category nationally and inspired the creation of more than 20 look-a-like products by other food manufacturers. More recently, Land O'Lakes introduced No•Fat Sour Cream, a revolutionary new product that's proving to be another hit — one that's also inspiring a host of imitators. The '80s also witnessed an increased marketing emphasis in cheese at Land O'Lakes. By far the majority of members' milk processed by Land O'Lakes goes into the production of cheese. During the 1980s, Land O'Lakes 4-Quart deli cheese line became the nation's number-one selling deli favorite.

If all of this couldn't get people's minds off butter, no problem. Land O'Lakes Sweet Cream Butter kept up its strength as the flagship of the organization's food line, becoming in 1985 Land O'Lakes first product available nationwide and remaining the country's number-one branded butter.

Good and lean

Lean Cream, with half the fat of
regular sour cream, was an
early low-fat offering. Consumers
today know the product by
its new name, Light Sour Cream.

ARNIE BERDAN:
A LONG-TIME RELATIONSHIP

When Arnie Berdan began working at United Farmers Cooperative in Lafayette, Minn., back in 1955, bottling milk and making butter were the co-op's main activities. Its feed business was small. But from the start of Berdan's career at United Farmers, one constant has been the co-op's steady relationship with Land O'Lakes.

Today the cooperative provides feed, seed, agronomy products and farm equipment to its 1,400 members, who raise everything from soybeans to hogs, and the creamery business is a fading memory. "Right when Land O'Lakes started manufacturing feed, we became one of the first cooperatives to supply members with Land O'Lakes Ag Service products," says Berdan, who's managed the co-op since 1957. "Over time Land O'Lakes research has developed better rations, adding strength to the feed business. It has really helped us as a local co-op that the regional organization invested

in that," he says. In addition to supplying ag products, Land O'Lakes has provided Livestock Production Specialists and other consultants who help farmer-members make the most of the products they buy. "To continue to grow, we need the business of all the local producers, large and small," Berdan says. "Land O'Lakes has taught our employees the product knowledge they need to serve all kinds of farmers."

Humor sells

In the 1980s, Land O'Lakes began using humor to advertise its milk replacer for pigs.

A pig saved is a pig earned.

LAND O LAKES₀ LitterMilk₀ can make the difference. Because it is different. It's formulated to save more baby pigs.
Land O' Lakes researchers tested LitterMilk against conventional milk replacers. They found that one-day-old pigs fed LitterMilk with PRT-99 had a survival rate 3.7 times greater than pigs on conventional milk replacer products despite the presence of E. coli scours-causing bacteria.
And, in field tests on 23 farms under practical conditions, pigs removed from sows and fed LitterMilk with PRT 99 had an 88% survival rate.
As part of an ongoing management program, LitterMilk works, and works hard. Because it leads to higher survival rates. More pigs per sow. And that translates into something you can bank on.
Try LitterMilk on your next farrowing. You'll wean more pigs.

LAND O LAKES
LITTERMILK

Circle 154 on Reply Card

Successful marketing

The number of animals consuming Land O'Lakes feeds increased 50 percent between 1986 and 1990.

Strength in agronomy

Land O'Lakes and Cenex each own 50 percent of the Cenex/Land O'Lakes Agronomy Co., which is supplied by CF Industries, an interregional cooperative and one of North America's largest and most successful plant food companies.

LAND O'LAKES AND CENEX

When the partnership between Land O'Lakes and Cenex became official on January 1, 1987 (with 95.4 percent of Land O'Lakes members voting in favor of it), both organizations predicted that the consolidation of Ag Services activities would save about $10 million in operational costs each year. This forecast was wrong. The actual savings were much greater — in the first years of the joint venture they were closer to $17 million annually.

Cenex, a St. Paul-based ag services cooperative formed in 1931, at the time served member co-ops in 13 states from Wisconsin to the West Coast. In addition to its role as a supplier of fertilizer, agricultural chemicals, feed, seed, and management services, Cenex was also a fully integrated energy company, with a full line of propane, diesel, lubricants and gasoline for producers and residents of rural communities. These strengths meshed well with those of Land O'Lakes. Not only did the consolidation bring about greater economies of scale, but it generated substantial gains in combined market share. For example, during the first five years of the venture, feed sales rose 57 percent for hogs, 60 percent for beef cattle, 73 percent for dairy cows, and 365 percent for poultry. Most important, the partnership demonstrated that two separate entities could work together and capitalize on their individual strengths. Local cooperatives and producers were the true winners.

Promotional materials for the Cenex/Land O'Lakes joint venture emphasized a common marketing approach to the country

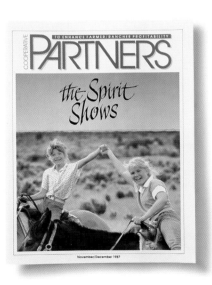

A new magazine

A third-generation member magazine arrived in 1987 in the form of *Cooperative Partners,* written for both Land O'Lakes and Cenex members.

Advances in crop protection

Imperial, Inc., a subsidiary of the Cenex/Land O'Lakes Agronomy Co., manufactures the Class line of crop protection products at a state-of-the-art facility near Hampton, Iowa.

You may recognize some of the ingredients in our new non-ionic surfactant.

New Preference™ non-ionic surfactant.

Put simply, it's the only product that amounts to a hill of beans. Introducing Preference, the only non-ionic surfactant made from soybean derivatives.

Many herbicide labels recommend adding a non-ionic surfactant to increase performance. In university and research farm tests, Preference performed as well or better than any non-ionic surfactant on the market.

And with each gallon you purchase, we'll make a donation to FoodWatch℠—the organization that delivers accurate information to the public about the food you grow.

Get new Preference today at your local Cenex/Land O'Lakes cooperative. Then use your crop to protect your crop.

™Trademark of Land O'Lakes, Inc.
℠Service mark of Agriculture Council of America.

CENEX LAND O LAKES CENEX

AgriSource
Information System for Crop Technology

Milk Value

Making pork production a science

Spectacular advances took place in hog farming during the 1980s and '90s, as producers became increasingly sophisticated in their use of swine genetics, feeding and farm management.

Practically the whole menagerie

Although Land O'Lakes feeding programs mostly focus on such animals as beef cattle, dairy cows and hogs, the organization also markets feeds for poultry, pets and exotic species.

Precision Agriculture

Crop-yield monitoring that makes use of computers and satellite technology is just one aspect of "Precision Agriculture" being employed by the Agronomy Co. and the Seed division.

Land O'Lakes Calf Milk Replacer — the first and the best

For all tastes

Land O'Lakes markets a wide variety of natural and process cheese — cheese for all occasions and tastes.

NEW PRODUCTS FOR NEW MARKETS

The food business is especially competitive — an enterprise in which small gains in market share are important, but where the introduction of new products is costly. As a member-owned cooperative, Land O'Lakes has made its mark by developing new products from its members' milk that creatively meet customer needs and that often fill previously unfilled niches in the marketplace. Land O'Lakes first such product was sweet cream butter. It was a tremendous success, and it remains a very important part of the Land O'Lakes foods line-up. So do other spreads and butter extensions — like Light Butter — that Land O'Lakes has developed over the years. But the primary food product for Land O'Lakes today is cheese. Upwards of 70 percent of Land O'Lakes members' milk goes toward cheese production. An important market for this cheese is the snack foods industry. Foodservice customers also are important to Land O'Lakes. In 1990 a survey of foodservice distributors ranked Land O'Lakes the nation's top supplier of cheese to hotels and restaurants.

Through its Country Lake Foods division, Land O'Lakes has opened up other new markets for its members' milk. Formed in 1988 by the consolidation of the Bridgeman, Lakeside Dairy, and Norris Creameries milk operations, Country Lake Foods specializes in expanding the market for milk, juices and cultured products. Its Tasty, Light and Creamy (TLC) line of reduced-fat products has earned high marks for flavor and freshness. The division has pioneered a number of other innovative products in recent years, including shelf-stable coffee creamers, extended shelf-life half and half, and the "Plus 3" line of products, which are fortified with vitamin E and natural cultures that aid in digestion.

Cheese production at the Land O'Lakes processing and packaging plant in Spencer, Wis.

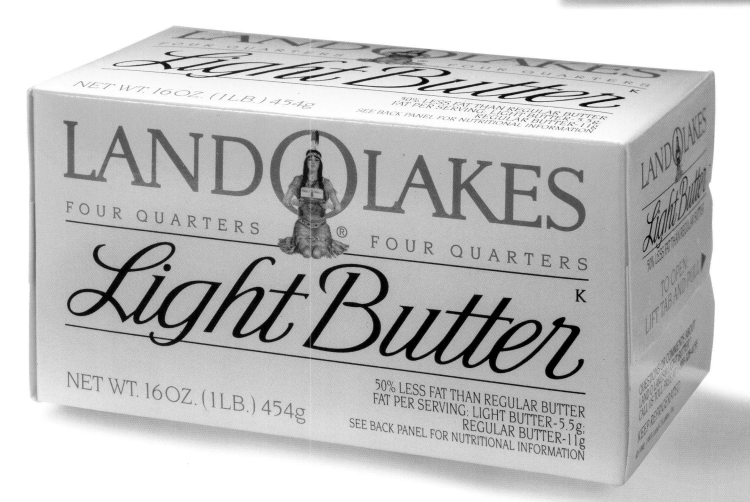

A growing line of spreads

Land O'Lakes Light Butter and Spread with Sweet Cream created new options for consumers seeking reduced-fat spreads.

The Cream of Spreads

Try the spread that has a dairy-fresh taste without the cholesterol.

Made with tradition, but made for today.

RANAE AND DWIGHT HASSELQUIST:
FARMERS WHO CHOOSE LAND O'LAKES

Ranae and Dwight Hasselquist, who own a dairy farm near Center City, Minn., could sell their milk to any of several dairy organizations in the region, but they have been steady Land O'Lakes producers since they went into business more than a decade ago. "We like Land O'Lakes because of the amount of work they do to develop dairy products that will sell," Dwight explains. "They're professional, forward-thinking, and self-reliant."

The couple, who have a 100-head dairy herd and also farm 200 acres of corn and hay, prefer selling their milk to a cooperative. "We both like to be involved in agriculture off the farm, and belonging to a co-op allows us to do that," says Ranae, who serves as a Land O'Lakes local unit delegate. "People who sell to private dairy organizations have absolutely no say as to how those businesses are run."

The Hasselquists recently expanded their dairy operation, tripling their herd size and adding new equipment. A Land O'Lakes Dairy Enterprise Consultant helped their business grow. "The consultant helped us with cash flow projections, and continues to advise us," Dwight says. As a result of the efficiency of their expanded operation, their lives — as well as those of their four young children — are better. "Our goals are not only to run a dairy farm that is profitable, but to have the freedom and flexibility for more family time," Dwight says.

Fluid milk and soft goods

The Country Lake Foods line includes many no- and low-fat products, as well as sour cream and other soft goods.

Knowledge for producers

Land O'Lakes programs to help dairy farmers run their businesses more profitably include the Dairy Enterprise Consulting Program and the Dairy Development Program.

The deli leader

A dedication to high quality has made Land O'Lakes the top marketer of deli cheese in the U.S.

Support and guidance

Land O'Lakes producers can tap the skills of agricultural experts though AgriSource and other co-op consulting services.

Cheese sauce in development at Land O'Lakes research facilities

THE CHALLENGES AHEAD

Creameries came together to form Land O'Lakes in 1921 to solve some specific problems — butter's high transport costs, erratic quality and the lack of a marketing plan. The organization quickly met those challenges, but new challenges kept coming. Keeping in mind its deep cooperative roots and the needs of its members, Land O'Lakes is prepared to make the most of the years ahead. Land O'Lakes vision, put simply, is to be one of the best food and agricultural companies in the world. The organization already is a leader in the production and marketing of Dairy Foods and Ag Service products, but accelerating changes in technology, communication and trade policies make the "present" seem to count for a shorter and shorter period of time. As Land O'Lakes President Jack Gherty is fond of saying, "Whatever you did to get you there is never enough to keep you there."

Land O'Lakes has grown and thrived for 75 years. That it has met its members' needs for three-quarters of a century testifies to the soundness of its philosophy and its resolve to stay true to its goals and mission. In the future lies a borderless world of trade, an agricultural economy with less government support, and constant change in production methods and technology. Land O'Lakes expects to keep growing, improving its performance, and building upon its reputation for quality in order to make that future a better place for all of its members.

Still more trucks

Like the trucks of the 1920s that were the first to bear the Land O'Lakes name, trucks still are being used to market Land O'Lakes products. This van is part of a marketing effort in California, the newest territory for Land O'Lakes butter.

The next generation

Land O'Lakes contributes part of its pretax earnings to help support the FFA, 4-H Clubs and other organizations that build leadership among rural youth.

A brisk day for business at the Hills, Minn., co-op, one of more than a thousand Land O'Lakes-affiliated member cooperatives in 15 states

On a screen near you

ProWare, a sophisticated animal feeding program, is being used by growing numbers of Land O'Lakes producers.

At the Land O'Lakes Silver Anniversary celebration in 1946, Dr. J.O. Christianson, head of the University of Minnesota School of Agriculture, described the founders of Land O'Lakes as "translators of dreams into reality." Those dreams were the product of people with vision — and they succeeded in creating a market- and customer-driven cooperative that, today, is committed to optimizing the value of its members' dairy, crop and livestock production. "The dream still lives," says Chairman Stan Zylstra.

"Our vision," says President Jack Gherty, "is to be one of the best food and agricultural companies in the world. If we do this, we will be our customers' first choice for products and services, and our employees' first choice for work. We also will be responsible to our owners and to rural America, and a leader in our communities."

Land O'Lakes has a heritage that is rich in rural values, family and respect for the land. Its cooperative roots run deep, and its values reflect the kind of organization it is and what it believes. Land O'Lakes believes in people and it believes in setting high standards of performance. Land O'Lakes also believes in customer commitment, quality and integrity. "With these values as our guide," says President Gherty, "we believe we will succeed both individually and as a company now and into the future."

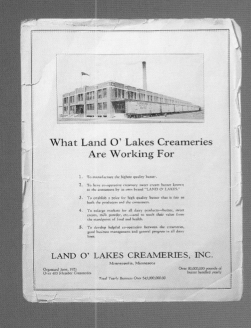

Board Chairman Stan Zylstra (left), and President Jack Gherty

An early Land O'Lakes mission statement from 1927

19**21**—19**96**

1921**
Gathering in St. Paul from all parts of Minnesota, 320 co-op creamery representatives vote to form the Minnesota Cooperative Creameries Association.

1924
After reviewing nearly 100,000 contest entries from around the country, the association's judges select "Land O'Lakes" as the new name to use in marketing members' butter.

1926
The association moves to a new headquarters building in Northeast Minneapolis.

1926
The name of the association's butter proves so popular that the membership votes to adopt Land O'Lakes Creameries, Inc., as the organization's new name.

1927
Land O'Lakes airs its first radio program on WCCO in the Twin Cities. The show features music and talks by company President John Brandt.

1927
The Land O'Lakes creamery in Little Falls, Minn., celebrates Charles Lindbergh's solo flight across the Atlantic by airlifting 40 pounds of butter to its native-son aviator.

1928
Land O'Lakes bolsters its product line with the addition of eggs and poultry.

1929
A new Feed department begins selling high-quality feeds for cattle, hogs, and poultry.

1930
Land O'Lakes strengthens a weakening butter market by purchasing 7 million pounds to stabilize prices.

1933
Land O'Lakes scrip money, backed by the organization's reserves in a year of financial depression and bank closings, helps member co-ops pay their dairy producers.

1934
With the arrival of Wisconsin's National Cheese Federation into the Land O'Lakes family, the organization launches its first significant efforts to market and grade cheese.

1937
At Luck, Wis., Land O'Lakes opens its first milk-drying plant, paving the way for the large-scale production of skim milk powder, casein and buttermilk powder during the war years ahead.

1940
The constant temperature and humidity of Mississippi River bluff limestone caves allows Land O'Lakes to begin production of aged cheese that will be marketed under the "Cavqurd" label.

1942
Many Land O'Lakes plants convert to the production of dried eggs, dried milk and other essential war goods.

1944
Annual production of 119 million pounds makes Land O'Lakes the nation's largest producer of dried milk powder.

1946
Land O'Lakes marks its 25th anniversary with the publication of its first history book and a celebratory Silver Anniversary annual meeting.

1948
A 187-acre plot of land in Anoka, Minn., becomes the organization's first experimental farm, where Land O'Lakes scientists test animal feeds, fertilizers, and feeds.

1950
The Margarine Act repeals federal restrictions on the coloring of margarine, and Land O'Lakes responds with a butter marketing campaign that soon carries sales to all-time highs.

1951
The introduction of Calf Milk Replacer gives farmers a high-quality substitute for the valuable skim milk they had been using to feed calves.

1952

In its first acquisition of another business, Land O'Lakes purchases Bridgeman Creameries. For the next three decades, the organization operates Bridgeman soda fountains and restaurants.

1953

An era ends with the death of longtime President and General Manager John Brandt.

1957

A new multi-purpose dairy plant opens in Mountain Lake, Minn., where a local co-op creamery had dissolved to enable members to become direct Land O'Lakes customers.

1958

For the first time, 100 percent of Land O'Lakes Grade A milk is procured from producers with bulk milk operations — a change made possible by members' steady replacement of milk cans with bulk tanks.

1963

The purchase of Dairy Belt Cheese and Butter Company of Spencer, Wis., gives Land O'Lakes the facilities to make a big entry into the cheese market.

1964

Land O'Lakes becomes a member of Central Farmers Fertilizer Company (today known as CF Industries), giving members access to a wide variety of plant foods.

1969

This is a peak year for acquisitions and mergers, with 37 organizations becoming part of the Land O'Lakes family.

1970

In a step that begins a tremendous growth in Ag Services, Land O'Lakes merges with Farmers Regional Cooperative (Felco) of Fort Dodge, Iowa.

1972

After extensive formulation and test marketing, Land O'Lakes margarine makes its debut.

1974

The Answer farm, a 535-acre ag research facility, opens near Fort Dodge, Iowa.

1980

On its way to becoming the nation's leading marketer of deli cheeses, Land O'Lakes introduces its 4-Quart cheese line.

1981

Land O'Lakes moves to a new corporate headquarters building in Arden Hills, Minn.

1981

Wisconsin's Lake to Lake Dairy Cooperative, with its strong consumer cheese presence in California and more than 1,300 member-owners, merges with Land O'Lakes.

1982

Land O'Lakes merges with Midland Cooperatives, a Minneapolis-based ag supply co-op that markets feed, seed, agronomy products and petroleum.

1987

An innovative joint venture with Cenex results in shared ownership of the Cenex/Land O'Lakes Agronomy Co. and a marketing effort that unifies the Feed and Seed operations owned by Land O'Lakes with the petroleum operations owned by Cenex.

1991

Land O'Lakes International Development activities involve 200 training courses and outreach programs with participants in 32 countries.

1992

Land O'Lakes introduces No•Fat Sour Cream — a fat-free product that soon becomes the number-one seller in its category.

1993

Land O'Lakes Western Feed division expands its operations as far west as Hawaii and Guam.

1996

The 75th Annual Meeting celebrates Land O'Lakes best year ever, with earnings in each core business exceeding plan.

LAND O'LAKES BOARD PRESIDENTS AND CHAIRMEN OF THE BOARD*

H.B. Nickerson
elected Board President
in 1921

John Brandt
elected Board President
in 1923

M.H. Mauritson
elected Board President
in 1953

Dan Holtz
elected Board President
in 1962

Melvin Sprecher
elected Board President
in 1970

Claire Sandness
elected Chairman of the
Board in 1977

Stan Zylstra
elected Chairman of the
Board in 1988

LAND O'LAKES CHIEF EXECUTIVE OFFICERS*

A.J. McGuire
was Organization Manager
until being named General
Manager in 1922

John Brandt
named General Manager
in 1933

Frank Stone
named General Manager
in 1953

Dave Henry
named General Manager
in 1967

Ralph Hofstad
named President in 1974

John E. Gherty
named President in 1989

*In 1972, the title "Board
President" was changed
to "Chairman of the Board,"
and the title "General
Manager" was changed to
"President."

LAND O'LAKES BOARD OF DIRECTORS—1995

Connie Cihak,
  Lonsdale, Minn.
Bob Cropp,*
  Oregon, Wis.
Les Deckert,
  Henning, Minn.
Richard Eltgroth,
  Sauk Centre, Minn.
Jim Fife,
  Wenatchee, Wash.
Paul Forey,
  Columbus, Neb.
Robert Gaebe,
  New Salem, N.D.
John Graff,
  LaSalle, Minn.
Gene Hager,
  St. Peter, Minn.
Norm Havel,
  Bondurant, Iowa
Ev Herness,
  Whitehall, Wis.
  (1st Vice Chairman)
Stan Kaczmarek,
  Green Bay, Wis.
Peter Kappelman,
  Manitowoc, Wis.
Paul Kent,
  Mora, Minn.
Kevin Kepler,
  Hillsboro, Wis.
George Koch,
  Puposky, Minn.
Oscar Lagerlund,
  Burlington, Wash.
Jim Lenz,
  Manson, Iowa
John Long,
  Gackle, N.D.

Jim Miller,
  Hardy, Neb.
Wes Moechnig,
  Lake City, Minn.
Murl Nord,
  Blackduck, Minn.
  (Secretary)
Bob Ode,
  Brandon, S.D.
Doug Reimer,
  Guttenberg, Iowa
Dean Roth,
  Boscobel, Wis.
C. Ford Runge,*
  St. Paul, Minn.
Ernie Salvog,
  Miltona, Minn.
John Siegmund,
  Kewaunee, Wis.
Jim Simmons,
  Buffalo, Minn.
Darwin Sittig,
  New Hampton, Iowa
Jim Sunde,
  Cherokee, Iowa
Floyd Timm,
  Wolsey, S.D.
Larry Wojchik,
  Clear Lake, Wis.
  (2nd Vice Chairman)
Bill Zuhlke,
  Markesan, Wis.
Stan Zylstra,
  Hull, Iowa
  (Chairman)

*Advisory members

LAND O'LAKES CORPORATE OFFICERS—1995

John E. Gherty,
  President and CEO
Duane Halverson,
  Executive Vice President and COO
Ron Ostby,
  Group Vice President,
  Finance & Planning and CFO
Dave Johnson,
  Cenex/Land O'Lakes Agronomy Co.
George Barr,
  Midwest Feed
Don Berg,
  Dairy Procurement/Membership
Jerry Booren,
  Western Feed
John Bottger,
  Spreads/Specialty Products Operations
Rex Carlson,
  Feed Marketing/Sales
Martha Cashman,
  International Development
Paul Christ,
  Dairy Analysis/Forecasting
Bob DeGregorio,
  Ag Research & Technology/
  Animal Milk Products
Moe Failer,
  Treasurer
Mike Fronk,
  Food Ingredients/Custom
  Products/Foodservice
Al Giese,
  Plant Food
Lynn Girouard,
  Consumer Foods
Dan Hanson,
  Planning & Development

Dave Hettinga,
  Research, Technology & Engineering
Doug Johnson,
  Dairy Foods Operations
Dan Knutson,
  Corporate Controller
Lawrie Kull,
  Dairy Membership
Jack Martin,
  Human Resources
Maury Miller,
  Member Services/Communications
Tom Packard,
  Milk/Ice Cream
John Rebane,
  General Counsel
Rita Page Reuss,
  Public Affairs
Paul Rhein,
  Crop Protection Products
Chuck Schmidt,
  Business Development
Dave Seehusen,
  Seed
John Swanson,
  Feed Operations
Gary Vanic,
  Cheese Operations
Tom Verdoorn,
  Dairy Foods Administration
Jim Wahrenbrock,
  Feed/Seed/Member Services
  Administration
Mark Wilberts,
  Information Systems

ACKNOWLEDGMENTS

The majority of the artifacts and photographs that appear in this book are from the collection of Land O'Lakes. Artifacts and historical photographs on the pages listed below were generously made available by the following individuals and organizations: Bruce Anthony—p.24; Barb Barth—p.41; Walter Cantley—p.64; Joe Ciannamea—pp. 28, 29, 98; Cokato Historical Society—pp. 9, 10, 16, 45; Dassel Cooperative Dairy Assn.—p. 31; Dr. Frank Crane—pp. 70, 78; Les Deckert—p. 21; Barb Dhein—pp. 47, 62, 63; Don Eck—p. 61; Lyle Eckberg—pp. 38, 41, 42, 50, 77; Kathy Fauth—pp. 53, 119; Patti Gliniecki—p. 47; Patty Halfmann—pp. 79, 80, 83, 90, 91; Joyce Harland—p. 61; Adeline Holtz—p. 130; Doug Horn—pp. 49, 50, 80; Jess Johnson—p.79; Judy Kahler—pp. 91, 99, 103; Bruce Kirking—p. 107; Jill Kohler—p. 59; Paul Lemke—p. 73; Library of Congress (Farm Security Administration Collection)—p. 62; Herb Mauritson—p. 130; Edna McKenna—p. 56; Minnesota Historical Society—pp. 10, 11, 12, 14, 16, 17, 18, 19, 22, 29, 40, 44, 45, 46, 54, 60, 63, 81; Virginia Nickerson—p. 130; Carolyn Patten—p. 87; Jill Porter—p. 103; Jim Simmons—p. 13; Laurinda Solseth—pp. 44, 61, 95; Stearns County Historical Society (Myron Hall Photo Collection)—pp. 45, 78, 82, 84; Nancy Thompson—pp. 29, 42, 61, 70; Darrel Van Amber—pp. 51, 71; Gary Weness—p. 69, Rollie Zeller—pp. 36, 43, 77.

AUTHOR: Jack El-Hai, a Minneapolis writer with special interests in history and business. **DESIGN:** Craig S. Davidson, CIVIC, Minneapolis. **PHOTOGRAPHY:** Eric Mortenson, St. Paul. **PROJECT MANAGER:** Steve Komula, Land O'Lakes, Inc. **PREPRESS:** Digit Imaging, Inc., Minneapolis. **PRINTING AND BINDING:** Friesens, Altona, Manitoba, Canada.

Values **THE LAND O'LAKES HERITAGE IS RICH IN RURAL VALUES, FAMILY AND RESF**

PRIDE, WE WILL CONTINUE OUR COMMITMENT TO SERVE FARMERS, RURAL AMERI

BELIEVE. PEOPLE: **WE BELIEVE IN PEOPLE — IN VALUING AND RECOGNIZING A WC**

BELIEVE IN SETTING HIGH STANDARDS — DEFINING CLEAR GOALS AND REWARDIN

MITMENT: **WE BELIEVE THE CUSTOMER IS FUNDAMENTAL TO OUR SUCCESS — WORK**

BELIEVE LAND O'LAKES STANDS FOR QUALITY — STRIVING TO MAKE OUR BEST BE

AND OPEN COMMUNICATION. WITH THESE VALUES AS OUR GUIDE, WE WILL PROVID